# CONTENTS

# The Parables

## Understanding What Jesus Meant

### GARY INRIG

Discovery House®

from Our Daily Bread Ministries

Printed in the United States of America

First printing of this edition in 2015

# DEDICATION

To Elizabeth

*whose life has been for me*

*a living parable displaying*

*the love of our God*

*and*

*in loving memory of*

Dr. Arthur Stinton

A s I have completed the work on this book, the Lord, in His grace, has taken us through the school of suffering, as my wife has undergone surgery for cancer. The God whom we meet in the parables has met us in our need, and we have learned again how wonderful our

God is. We have also gained a new appreciation for the family of God. The believers at Bethany Chapel in Calgary, Alberta, Canada, and Reinhardt Bible Church in Dallas, Texas, heard some of these chapters as sermons. Now they have been living them back to us as agents of God's love. How we thank God for them.

I owe a special debt of gratitude to Jeanette Abercrombie and Glenese Hensarling for their careful work in preparing the manuscript.

Special thanks are due to Elizabeth, who is truly God's good favor to me (Prov. 18:22), and to Janice, Stephen, and Heather, three who bring joy to their parents (Prov. 10:1).

# PREFACE

The American playwright Arthur Miller, almost as famous for his play *Death of a Salesman* as for his brief marriage to Marilyn Monroe, once observed, "In every successful drama there is something which makes a person say, 'Hey! that's *me!*' " The story becomes a mirror in which self-recognition produces self-understanding.

Many of the stories the Lord Jesus told have precisely that effect. To read them properly is to see ourselves. But they are more than mirrors. They almost always become windows into the heart and mind of God himself. As a result, they do far more than reveal who we are. They help us know who God is. They not only expose our condition, but also point to a divine remedy. Self-recognition without a divine provision would bring only discouragement. The Lord's parables bring encouragement, because in them we meet ourselves and our God.

Not all of Jesus' parables were intended to be mirrors for those who heard them. Sometimes the Lord used parables as veils. They served to hide the truth from people whose response to Him indicated that they were under divine judgment. This is especially true of the parables of Matthew 13, as Jesus makes clear in verses 10–13. But the parables we will consider in this book are not of that character. The stories dealt with here were intended not to hide but to illumine.

Three general comments are important as we begin our study. First, the parables are not isolated stories. They were nearly always told to answer a question or address a particular situation. It is therefore very important to study the context in which the biblical authors place them. Much recent scholarship has sought to isolate the parables from their biblical context, to seek an original setting "behind the text" or in the life of the early church. But such conjecture distorts the purpose of the Holy Spirit. The parables can only be understood in the context of written Scripture. Second, the Lord's stories are parables, not allegories. Although details may have symbolic significance, more commonly a parable is intended to teach one main point. Therefore, we need to seek to grasp that truth firmly and not wander in the lush forest of speculation, trying to assign "meaning" to secondary details. Third, as we read these stories, we need consciously to leave our twentieth-century Western world. Jesus' stories draw on the common daily life of first-century Palestine. To hear Him properly, we need to smell the aroma of Jewish villages and feel the dust of Galilean roads. As we seek to enter that world, these stories will come alive with energizing freshness.

We are told that familiarity breeds contempt. It probably doesn't where the parables are concerned. But familiarity does breed complacency. Because we think we know these stories, we do not really listen to them. So now, as we sit again at the feet of our Lord to listen to His wonderful words, we must try to listen as though for the first time.

# CHAPTER ONE

# KNOWING MY FATHER

A. W. Tozer begins his masterly study of the character of God, *The Knowledge of the Holy*, with a provocative sentence: "What comes into our minds when we think about God is the most important thing about us." For some, such a claim seems to be pious rhetoric, the kind of thing a preacher is expected to say on Sunday morning. God-talk may have its place, but in the real world other things seem far more relevant. The agenda of modern secular man has little place for God. I remember a philosophy student insisting to me that life's really important questions weren't related to God at all, but to such things as the nuclear issue, environmental crises, economic dislocation, political upheaval, and personal matters of self-worth and personal dignity.

For others, Tozer's words have a ring of truth. What I think about God *is* important. In fact, those other questions can only be answered in the light of who He is and what He says. But that creates a dilemma. In the theological cafeteria of the twentieth century, which God should I choose? Or should I build my own God *à la carte*, combining ideas that seem to me to be palatable or appealing? From where do I get my understanding of God?

For still others, the response is one of applause. Tozer is right. We must be God-centered, and what we think about God is not just important, it is all-important. At the same time, we have a sneaking suspicion that those who speak most confidently about God are often woefully ignorant of Him. After all, history is replete with atrocities and absurdities done in His name by those who claim to be carrying out His will. And recent events have exposed the enormous difference between the public image and private reality of some self-appointed spokespersons for God.

I have no doubt that the Lord Jesus would have agreed with Tozer emphatically. What enters our minds when we think about God really is the most important thing about us. Over and over, Christ sought to scrape away the residue of misinformation and misunderstanding that obstructed people's view of His Father. But He also makes it clear that knowledge of God is not equivalent to theological orthodoxy, important as that is. The evidence that we know God is not so much our ability to define the divine attributes, **as** it is our response to people. Right knowledge of God is present when we imitate our Father's response.

That is the theme of one of His most familiar and powerful stories. We know it as the parable of the prodigal son, but that convenient name indicates that we have perhaps not listened to it carefully enough. For the story tells not of one son but of two, and the Lord's purpose is not so much to describe a prodigal son as His Father's love. It is, in fact, the parable of the Father's heart, recorded in Luke 15.

## The Question about the Lord's Disreputable Companions

To appreciate the story, it is particularly important that we see the events that inspired it. Therefore, we begin with Luke 15:1–2:

> Now the tax collectors and "sinners" were all gathering around to hear him. But the Pharisees and the teachers of the law muttered, "This man welcomes sinners and eats with them."

The dust of the centuries has often obscured for us how consistently and deliberately the Lord Jesus shocked His contemporaries. His words and His actions persistently offended the religious and the self-righteous, and I suspect His behavior would have made many of us uncomfortable as well.

One of the surprises of the gospels is their account of the very unlikely people who were drawn to Jesus. "Tax collectors and sinners" represented, to the Pharisees, the dregs of society. To us, the words "tax collectors" conjure up unpleasant feelings about high taxes, indecipherable bureaucratic jargon, and the fear of an audit. But in our Lord's time, tax collectors were not merely unpopular. As agents of the hated Roman oppressor, they were pariahs. The system of taxation made corruption prevalent, and abuse of power was commonplace. Because they dealt so often with Gentiles, tax collectors were religiously "unclean," as well. Honest Jews could only regard such people as disloyal, dishonest, and disreputable. "Sinners" were of the same ilk. As the Pharisees used the term, it did not necessarily describe notorious sinners. More commonly it referred to ordinary people who lived with indifference to the rigorous observances of the pious. The religious derisively called them *am h'aretz*, "the people of the land," the non-observant, the unclean.

They may have been indifferent to religion, but such people were not indifferent to spiritual truth. They were drawn to the Lord's teaching—a fact that infuriated "the Pharisees and the teachers of the law," men who represented the epitome of religion and respectability in Jewish life. The problem was not so much sinful people's response to the Lord, but the Lord's response to them. After all, who could object if sinners came to learn? As long as they knew their place! But Jesus didn't merely tolerate their presence. "This man welcomes sinners." They felt comfortable in His presence! "And eats with them." In a culture where sharing a meal meant acceptance and even approval, how could a good man behave like this? How could He enjoy their company and have them enjoy His? "That tells us all we need to know about Jesus. You can tell a man by the company He keeps, and since He's not with good people, He's obviously not a good man."

The religious leaders were people who claimed to know God and who were offended by the kind of people Jesus attracted. They are not alone in having these feelings. If we are honest with ourselves, we sometimes share their attitude. Not everyone who follows Jesus is "our kind of person." It is precisely this prejudice that leads to what follows: "Then Jesus told them this parable." In fact, He tells them three parables—about a lost sheep, a lost coin, and a lost son. And each parable is addressed to the self-righteous Pharisees, putting a mirror before them and opening a window into heaven. They, in fact, know far less about both themselves and God than they think they do.

There is an ancient story about a young man who came to a rabbi he greatly admired. "Sir, I love you, and I want to follow you. May I become your disciple?" "My son," came the reply, "do you know what hurts me and gives me pain?" "No, sir, I don't think I do." "Then how can you say you love me, if you don't know what hurts me?"

That is the sense of these three parables. How can we say we know God if we do not know what gives Him pain and brings Him joy? The Lord wants us to see that the Father's heart hurts for the lost and rejoices when the lost are found. He uses a concept we all understand. When something of value is lost, we do not despise it, we search for it, and rejoice in the finding of it. It is obvious that people feel this way, but the amazing discovery is that God does also. That is the point of the parables. They tell us not so much about a lost sheep as a seeking shepherd, not so much about a lost coin as a searching woman, not so much about a lost son as a loving father. And all these speak of our Father in heaven.

All three of these familiar stories are beautiful, but our focus here is on the third parable of Luke 15, which is one story told in two parts. This is an important observation that is often ignored. The Savior's story does not end with the return of the prodigal, but with the appeal to the older brother, and it is in the last half of the parable that the most powerful application is found, the one intended for the scribes and Pharisees.

## The Wayward Son and the Welcoming Father (Luke 15:11–24)

> Jesus continued: "There was a man who had two sons. The younger one said to his father, 'Father, give me my share of the estate.' So he divided his property between them.

"Not long after that, the younger son got together all he had, set off for a distant country and there squandered his wealth in wild living. After he had spent everything, there was a severe famine in that whole country, and he began to be in need. So he went and hired himself out to a citizen of that country, who sent him to his fields to feed pigs. He longed to fill his stomach with the pods that the pigs were eating, but no one gave him anything.

"When he came to his senses, he said, 'How many of my father's hired men have food to spare, and here I am starving to death! I will set out and go back to my father and say to him: Father, I have sinned against heaven and against you. I am no longer worthy to be called your son; make me like one of your hired men.' So he got up and went to his father.

"But while he was still a long way off, his father saw him and was filled with compassion for him; he ran to his son, threw his arms around him and kissed him.

"The son said to him, 'Father, I have sinned against heaven and against you. I am no longer worthy to be called your son.'

"But the father said to his servants, 'Quick! Bring the best robe and put it on him. Put a ring on his finger and sandals on his feet. Bring the fattened calf and kill it. Let's have a feast and celebrate. For this son of mine was dead and is alive again; he was lost and is found.' So they began to celebrate."

I haven't lost any sheep, but I have scoured the neighborhood searching for our wandering poodle, with my children in panic at the thought that she may be gone forever. And I have turned the house upside down looking for the diamond that had fallen out of my wife's engagement ring. We found the dog but not the diamond. But what can compare with the anguish of a parent's heart over a lost son? There is a horrible panic when an infant vanishes, a different but real panic when a grown child wanders morally or spiritually. The problem in the latter situation isn't that we don't know where they are or what they are doing, but that we do. We know they are in the far country, not only wasting their money but wasting their lives. Perhaps it is only a parent in such pain who can enter fully into the mood of this story.

### Leaving the Father's House (15:11–12)

Late in the summer of 1986 I drove with my father from Portland, Oregon, to Vancouver, B.C. Two years earlier my mother had died, and my father had known deep loneliness since then. He was not a man who found it easy to talk about his emotions, but on that trip he began to talk about his funeral and his finances. He died nine months later, and I am glad for the memory. But at the time, I was terribly uncomfortable. I didn't want to talk about *my* inheritance or what his death would mean for me financially. The money was his, and I wanted him to use it for himself. Anything else seemed disrespectful and grasping. And I wanted him to think about living, not about dying.

If we feel that way, we can guess that people in the Lord's time did too. This young man's request is a dagger in his father's heart. He doesn't want a loan, he wants his inheritance. "If you won't hurry up and die, give me what's

coming now. I want it, and I won't wait for it."
The Lord wants us to feel the shock of that
request. Some experts in Middle Eastern
culture tell us that the young man was virtually
expressing a wish for his father to die. A father
could initiate a discussion about inheritance,
but never a son. "To my knowledge in all
of Middle Eastern literature (aside from this
parable) from ancient times to the present, there
is no case of any son, older or younger, asking
for his inheritance from a father who is in good
health" (Kenneth Bailey, *Poet and Peasant*).

I can't imagine that the father meekly
followed his son's request. He knew his
son's character, and he knew his intentions.
Undoubtedly he tried to dissuade him. But
his son persisted. Heartsick, the father finally
relented. Sometimes a parent is helpless to
prevent a course of life leading to destruction.
There comes a time to let the prodigal go. So he
divided the estate, with two-thirds going to the
older brother and one-third to the younger, as
Jewish law required. Apparently the father went
beyond usual practice, because he distributed
not only his capital but also his property. This
was no small matter. After all, this represented

the old man's security for the future. He was now totally vulnerable.

### Living in the Far Country (15:13–16)

The young man is determined to be totally independent. When the text tells us that he "got together all he had," it suggests that he turned all his assets into ready cash. He sold the property, because he intended to cut all ties with his past and his parents. And he left behind not only his father's house, but also his father's God. "A distant country" can only mean Gentile country, characterized by pagan values and heathen morals. It takes little imagination to realize how he "squandered his wealth in wild living." He scattered his money like a sower scatters seed, and his crop was dissipation, "wild living." Back home few had any doubt that he was "squandering [his] property with prostitutes" (15:30).

Sooner or later, choices bring consequences. And so here. The young man runs out of money and into a famine. The good life is soon only a memory, and finally the realities of life drive him to desperation and even degradation. A local citizen hires him to feed pigs, a task unthinkable for a proud Jew. But desperation knows no pride, and the young man not only lives with the pigs, but is willing to eat with them. The fodder of pigs looks enticing. But in a time of famine pigs are more valuable than people, and so "no one gave him anything."

Had the Lord stopped at this point, his critics would have risen up with enthusiastic approval. "That's right. That's what happens to a sinner. He ends up degraded, with the stench of pigs upon him. He's getting what he deserves." But the Lord did not end there. The Pharisees were content to leave sinners in the pigpen. The Savior wants them to find the way back to the Father's house.

### Looking in the Mirror (15:17–19)

In a striking way, the Lord describes the turning point. Literally, He tells us that the young man "came to himself," or as we more commonly say, "he came to his senses." There is an insanity to sin, and this boy suddenly saw himself as he really was. The first step to spiritual sanity is repentance, a return to a realistic understanding of who God is and who we are in relation to Him. The young man realized that his choices had been sinful, against God and against his father. ("Father, I have sinned against heaven and against you.")

In accepting the responsibility for his actions and recognizing the wrong he had done, he embraced truth.

Undoubtedly, the young man's anthem when he left home had been, "I've gotta be me. I've gotta find myself." But we can never find ourselves in sinful indulgence. There is often more truth in the pigpen of consequences than in the banquet halls of revelry. The prodigal had left home to find his freedom. Instead he had found servitude, a bondage far worse than anything his father's hired men experienced. Sadly, it is often not until we reach the pigpen that we come to understand the glory of the Father's house.

But the boy's proposal indicates that, while he desires the father's house, he doesn't understand the father's heart. He knows he has forfeited all right to sonship. The best he hopes for is that his father may accept him as a hired servant. He is aware that he can claim nothing more.

### Learning about the Father (15:20–24)

There is no harder place to go than where you have failed. Villages can be cruel places. This boy's actions had been the talk of the town, and he knew that going home meant

running a gauntlet of criticism and hostility.
To come home bearing the smell of pigs and
wearing the rags of failure was the ultimate
humiliation. He had left town so sure of himself
and his future! But if that was the price, it had
to be paid. So he returned, not merely to home,
but to his father.

And then, as the Lord tells the story, we
realize the most amazing fact of all! This father
is no austere figure who has disowned his son
and shut him out of his heart. While the boy
is still a long way off, the father sees him. The
implication is astonishing. Here is a father who
is not only willing to receive his son, he has
been looking for him! Day after day, he has
been waiting for this moment. At a distance that
only a broken heart can leap, he recognizes his
son and instinctively realizes his need. Only a
broken man would run as his son is walking!
And he "was filled with compassion for him."
Note the timing. The son is too far away to
express his repentance, but already the father's
grace is present.

To understand the story, we need to know
that older men in the Middle East do not run.
This father was an aged and wealthy landowner.
Robes made running difficult, and the concept

of dignity made it inappropriate. Even in our time, important people restrain their emotions publicly. They may jog for exercise; they rarely race in excitement. But this father's heart is filled with two things: love for his son and a desire to reach him before any of the judgmental villagers do. Suddenly, the villagers are startled by the sight of this dignified man bolting through town to throw himself upon a dusty, ragged stranger and to smother him with kisses.

The son begins to pour out his well-rehearsed speech. "Father, I have sinned . . ." He gets no further. That is all the old man needs to hear. He turns to the crowd that has followed and gathered around to watch. Strikingly, he says nothing to his son; his actions will say it all. "Quick! Bring the best robe and put it on him." That would have been the father's festival robe worn on grand occasions; the boy was to be the guest of honor! "Put a ring on his finger"— not just as an ornament but as a symbol of authority. ". . . and sandals on his feet." Slaves and servants went barefoot. The father isn't merely clothing his son; he is covering him with honor and acceptance. "Bring the fattened calf" (the one carefully prepared for a special occasion) "and celebrate. For this son of mine was dead and is alive again; he was lost and is found." Nothing is to be ordinary. His prodigal son is to receive the highest honor.

There is a Buddhist story that provides a fascinating contrast to the Lord's story. It also tells of a son who left home and returned years later in rags and misery. His degradation was so profound that he did not recognize his own father. But his father recognized him and told the servants to take him into the mansion and to clean him up. The father, his identity unrevealed, watched his son's response. Gradually, time wrought changes, and the son became dutiful, considerate, and moral. Satisfied, the father finally revealed his identity and formally accepted his son as his heir.

The Pharisees would have understood and approved of such a story. It makes sense to wait for a son to achieve worthiness. It is reasonable to treat a repentant person according to the stage of penance achieved. But that is not the Father our Lord describes. It is not a parable of merits. Here is a picture of grace. God is not an austere being, impassively dispensing justice. He does not merely smile benignly upon the good and the righteous. His grace is almost undignified in its exuberance.

Here is a God who runs and rejoices and embraces. Here is a God who not only accepts the dry-cleaned and the sanitized, but who runs to the filthy, wayward son who has turned his heart toward home. Here is a God who, as time will make clear, gives not His best robe but His only Son. Here is a God who shouts to the returning rebel, "Welcome home!"

God celebrates over the dead child who has come to life, over the lost who is found. He doesn't merely accept the prodigal son, He rejoices with him and over him. But this is a God the Pharisees did not know. And that is why the story does not end with verse 24. In fact, the key to the story is what follows.

## The Respectable Brother and the Rejoicing Father (Luke 15:25–32)

"Meanwhile, the older son was in the field. When he came near the house, he heard music and dancing. So he called one of the servants and asked him what was going on. 'Your brother has come,' he replied, 'and your father has killed the fattened calf because he has him back safe and sound.'

"The older brother became angry and refused to go in. So his father went out and pleaded with him. But he answered his father, 'Look! All these years I've been slaving for you and never disobeyed your orders. Yet you never gave me even a young goat so I could celebrate with my friends. But when this son of yours who has squandered your property with pros-titutes comes home, you kill the fat-tened calf for him!'

" 'My son,' the father said, 'you are always with me, and everything I have is yours. But we had to celebrate and be glad, because this brother of yours was dead and is alive again; he was lost and is found.' "

### The Anger of the Older Brother (15:25–28a)

If the prodigal son is meant to represent the tax collectors and sinners of verse 1, it is obvious that the older brother is the Lord's portrait of the Pharisees of verse 2. Here is the hard-working, respectable son. When the villagers had criticized the wayward son, they had been warm, no doubt, in their praise of the dutiful son. He was a credit to his father, the one who had done the right thing.

Certainly the Lord is not criticizing goodness and respectability. But as Mark Twain said in his typically sardonic way: "Having spent considerable time with good people, I can understand why Jesus liked to be with tax collectors and sinners." There is a "goodness" that is not good and a "righteousness" that is not right. This older brother appeared to have a relationship with his father which, in fact, he did not have, and the Lord used him to unmask the Pharisees' claims truly to know the Father.

The sounds of celebration fall on very unsympathetic ears as the elder brother returns home. Music and dancing are not what he desires in his father's house. And the news he receives confirms his worst suspicions. His brother has returned—that good-for-nothing whom he despises—and his father has gone off the deep end in his celebration.

There is no doubt about the son's duty here. The oldest son should act as his father's special assistant on such occasions, as a co-host. This brother has no intention of playing such a role. "The older brother became angry and refused to go in." This is a studied insult to his father. Publicly he makes clear his disapproval of his father's actions. Like a teenager picking a fight with his parents before a house full of guests, he behaves in a way that is not only hurtful but humiliating. But there is even more here. *This son would rather not have fellowship with his father than accept his father's treatment of his brother.* He will not accept someone who has been the companion of pigs and prostitutes. If that costs him fellowship with his father, so be it.

The relevance of this to the context of Luke 15 is obvious. The Pharisees would not have fellowship with Jesus because of His treatment of people the Pharisees considered prodigals. Thus, they were putting themselves outside the Father's house. Refusal to accept all those whom the Lord accepts is no small matter. It reveals our relationship to God himself.

### The Plea of the Seeking Father (15:28b)

The father could have sent out a servant to order his son inside. Certainly a father in the Middle East had such authority: "We'll talk about it later, but not now. Get inside, smile, and do your job. But don't do this—not now, not this way. We deal with matters like this behind closed doors."

But the father who humbled himself to run to the returning prodigal humbles himself to appeal to the angry older brother. He "went out and pleaded with him." His love for this son is no less profound than his love for his other son. He does not stand on his dignity, but reveals his vulnerability.

### The Complaint of the Older Brother (15:29–30)

The older son has only contempt for such a response. In the light of the father's appeal, the heart of the son is exposed. He speaks angry words that reveal who he really is. Appearances suggest a son respectful of his father, totally different from his rebellious brother; anger unveils attitudes every bit as contemptible as the attitudes that led his brother to leave home. In fact, what we learn about this older brother may explain why the younger brother wanted to go to the far country!

The older brother has an attitude of *contempt for his father*. The "Look!" of verse 29 is full of disrespect, as is the litany of complaints. Clearly he has rehearsed these in his mind over the years, carefully calculating and storing up his grievances. He hasn't stayed home because he loved his father, but because working in his fields was a way to get what he wanted. He has shared his father's house but not his father's heart. At the same time, he is full of *contempt for his brother.* "This son of yours" says volumes. He will not accept him as "my brother." In his heart, he has written him out of the family and out of his life.

But despite his protestations, this man is more like his younger brother than he realizes. He is full of *concern for himself.* He is intensely self-centered, judging things only by how they satisfy his own interest. He cares nothing for his father's longings or his brother's needs. He is self-indulgent and resentful, angry that his father has not catered to his wishes. Most of all, he is no better than a servant. "All these years I've been slaving for you." He knows nothing of the joy of being a son. The younger brother was willing to become a servant; this son has been one in heart all along. He now stands exposed. This respectable son is, in fact, a rebel, lost in his father's house. He is so close to the father and yet so far from him.

What a penetrating portrait of the self-righteous and the religious! Morally respectable and publicly approved, such a person may be much farther from the Father than the prodigal in the pigpen.

### The Choice of the Older Brother (15:31–32)

The father's grace persists despite this outburst. A normal father would be furious at such an attack. But this father is different. He explains carefully, and says, in effect, "We had to celebrate and be glad; we had no choice. Because of who I am, a father, I rejoice over lost sons who return. Joy is the only possibility. Not to rejoice would be to deny who I am." The father is clear. He will not cancel the party, because he cannot. He is a gracious father who rejoices over children found.

Neither will the heavenly Father cancel the celebration. His heart aches, too, over the lost son—whether he is partying in the far country or working in the family's fields. When sinners repent and come home, He must welcome them with outstretched arms, and He must share a joyful meal with them. What Jesus is doing with tax collectors and sinners (15:1–2)

is what the Father does in heaven. The ⟨
the Lord Jesus and the grace of God are t⟨
themes of this story.

But there is a fascinating omission in the story. There is no ending. Did the older brother enter or not? We are not told because that is precisely the issue the Lord sets before the Pharisees and before us. To reject the Father's gracious treatment of the most unworthy of sinners is to deceive ourselves about our need for grace and to forfeit the fellowship with God that is based on grace alone. As long as the Pharisees stayed angry at the grace shown to sinners, they stood outside the Father's house.

The awful possibility is that we, too, can be in the Father's fields as servants but not really in His house as sons or daughters. We may be moral and respectable, but, because we have never truly known the Father who is loving, gracious, and welcoming, we are "older brothers." To such, the Father's appeal is "Come in."

Or we may be in the far country, scattering the resources of which He is ultimately the Giver. Perhaps the money has run out and the famine has come in, and we have reached the pigpen. We despair of ever being accepted in the Father's house. To all such, the Lord's story shouts, "Come home."

The bottom line is this. What we know of God is seen in how we view ourselves as lost and how we deal with others as lost. God's heart aches over those who are lost; God's heart rejoices over those who are found. How well we know Him is revealed by whether or not we ache and rejoice as He does.

# CHAPTER TWO

# LOVING MY NEIGHBOR

In the summer of 1988, controversy swirled around the release of the movie, *The Last Temptation of Christ*. Christians complained rightfully that the movie conveyed a distorted picture of the Lord Jesus, not only in a notorious dream sequence of sexual temptation, but in a consistent misrepresentation of Him as "Messiah without a cause," a man plagued by self-doubt and uncertainty. But the director, Martin Scorsese, kept insisting that people were missing the point. The movie, he claimed, wasn't intended for people who took the Bible literally, but for people who wanted to think about the "Jesus story" in a fresh way. He said viewers should recognize that, despite the film's unorthodox means, the essence of the story of Christ remained unharmed. "The message of Jesus' life is love."

The problem was not merely that Scorsese didn't take the Bible literally. Tragically he did not even take it seriously. He presents a Jesus who never existed, a figment of Nikos

Kazantzakis's fertile imagination. But suppose we were to grant Scorsese's thesis and reduce the gospel to "the message of Jesus' life is love." Having said that, what have we said? Joseph Fletcher became the spokesman for a "new morality" in his book *Situation Ethics*. He contended that love was the only criterion for morality. But as one reviewer observed, the word *love* runs through his book "like a greased pig." Always there, it is always elusive. The problem with a word like "love" is that it is so easily cheapened. It is the word of the seducer and the word of the huckster, but also the word of the sacrificial parent and the marriage partner.

There can be no doubt that "love" was a central part of Jesus' message. The story of the prodigal son certainly is a story about the love of God for all of us sinners, a love we are to share. Throughout the gospels we hear Him calling us to love God and to love others. Martin Luther properly observed that "A Christian is someone who lives outside himself. He lives in Christ by faith and in his neighbor by love." But the Lord Jesus refuses to allow His call to love to degenerate into a sentimental slogan. He modeled love in His life, and He describes love in one of the most powerful stories ever told, a story we know as the parable of the good Samaritan as found in Luke 10. The setting of that story is, however, often neglected. Yet it is crucial to a proper understanding of our Lord's message.

> On one occasion an expert in the law stood up to test Jesus. "Teacher," he asked, "what must I do to inherit eternal life?"
>
> "What is written in the Law?" he replied. "How do you read it?"
>
> He answered: " 'Love the Lord your God with all your heart and with all your soul and with all your strength and with all your mind'; and, 'Love your neighbor as yourself.' "
>
> "You have answered correctly," Jesus replied. "Do this and you will live."
>
> But he wanted to justify himself, so he asked Jesus, "And who is my neighbor?"
>
> (Luke 10:25–29)

As a ten-year-old boy, I went to summer camp for the first time. One of the boys in my cabin was significantly smaller than the rest of us, and, with the cruelty of children, we teased him endlessly. Our counselor, a wise old man of at least eighteen, intervened with a proposal. "Listen. You keep saying how small Alan is. I'll make you a deal. You let Alan hit you in the stomach as hard as he can, and then you can hit me as hard as you want." My cohorts faded into silence, but to me it sounded like a great deal. Obviously Alan wasn't big enough to break an egg, and I could already picture my football-playing counselor gasping from the power of my blow.

Or so I dreamed. Alan hit me so hard that I thought I would die. When I could finally breathe again, my time of glory came. I wound up and hit my counselor's stomach with all the power I could muster—and almost broke my fist! He didn't even squeak! I walked away with an aching stomach, sore knuckles, and severely wounded pride.

I think of that episode when I read the Lord's parables. They have a kick in them that leaves us rubbing our wounds and reflecting on the lessons. Certainly the man who came to the Lord expecting to score a knockout punch went away in a very different frame of mind.

## The Priority of Love: The Great Questions

The Lord's interrogator is "an expert in the law." But it is Jewish religious law, not Roman civil law in which he has expertise. In other words, this man is a theologian rather than an attorney. His motivation is transparent—to test Jesus. His is not the question of a sincere seeker but of an adversary inspecting Jesus, probing Him to expose suspected inadequacy. This man represents the religious establishment, which is troubled by the growing popularity of this unorthodox and unapproved teacher.

But if his motivation is dubious, his question is crucial: "Teacher, what must I do to inherit eternal life?" What question can be more important? There is a significant assumption to the query that this man shares with multitudes of others. Eternal life, he believes, is obtained by doing a set number of meritorious acts. Salvation comes by human works.

Intriguingly, the Lord doesn't quibble by pointing out the contradiction implicit in the man's question. You can't *do* something to inherit a gift. Inheritance is based on relationship, not achievement. Nor does He answer the question. Instead, He turns the man's question back on him and directs him to the Old Testament as the basis of authority. "What is written in the Law? How do you read it?" Swiftly but surely, the Lord has reversed the roles. The questioned has become the questioner, the hunted has become the hunter.

The theologian has asked life's greatest question. He now puts his finger on the heart of Old Testament theology to describe life's greatest need. First he quotes Deuteronomy 6:5: "Love the LORD your God with all your heart and with all your soul and with all your strength." And he combines this with Leviticus 19:18: "Love your neighbor as yourself."

This is a brilliant answer. Deuteronomy 6 is the heart of Old Testament faith, a passage that calls for undivided loyalty to Yahweh. Leviticus 19:18 captures the essence of the Holiness Code, an expression of God's will for His people. This is, in fact, the same answer the Lord gives to His critics in Matthew 22:34–40. This linking of the two verses is not found previously in the rabbinic tradition, and it seems entirely possible that the theologian is repeating what he has heard Jesus himself say. Biblical faith does not involve primarily a series of ritual acts, but a heart relationship to God, which shapes every facet of life. And this relationship to God is inseparable from our relationships to people around us.

The Lord readily accepts the man's answer. "You have answered correctly; do this and you will live." But something in the Lord's answer troubles the theologian. The theologian wants a list of rules that people can keep. Jesus prescribes a relationship to God that shapes life. Eternal life is not earned by works; it is received in a heart relationship with God.

This is no longer an intellectual game of cut and thrust. The discussion has become intensely personal and the questioner now finds himself the one under scrutiny. "But he wanted to justify himself." Something in the Savior's manner has put him on the defensive. Undoubtedly, he has felt the power of the command: Love God; love your neighbor. That is far different from a simple set of rules and works. Honesty would have driven him to admit his self-doubt: "That's my problem. I can't love God or my neighbor like that. I try but I fall short. I need help."

That kind of self-revelation, however, is too threatening even to consider. And so, wanting to get off the hook, he uses a diversionary tactic:

ask another question. Wishing to justify himself, he says to Jesus, "And who is my neighbor?"

While there is no doubt that his question is an evasion, it also represents a serious moral problem. If there is a neighbor I must love, is there also a non-neighbor I do not need to love? Do I have to love everyone? Where do I draw the line? The rabbis had explored this issue. Leviticus 19:18 uses the term "neighbor" as a synonym for "brother" or "people," and so the rabbis taught that one's neighbor was a fellow Israelite. Some Jewish scholars saw even further limits. The command, they said, applied to full proselytes, but not Samaritans or foreigners. Others were certain that "neighbor" excluded still more people: "A rabbinical saying ruled that heretics, informers, and renegades should be pushed into the ditch and not pulled out" (J. Jeremias, *Rediscovering the Parables,* p.159) The Essenes required that a member of the community should hate "all the sons of darkness," meaning even fellow Jews who were not part of their group.

It is easy to be critical of this kind of attitude, but it is far more common than we care to admit. Our newspapers are full of stories of people whose plights are ignored by passers-by. We live in a world drowning in human needs—the hurting, the homeless, the hungry. What are the limits to my love? How far does my responsibility go? Who isn't my neighbor? Who don't I have to love? These are hardly irrelevant questions in a world where "compassion fatigue" has reached epidemic proportions. The Lord's answer comes, not in the form of a lecture, but as a now-familiar and famous story.

## The Portrait of Love: The Good Samaritan

> In reply Jesus said: "A man was go-
> ing down from Jerusalem to Jeri-
> cho, when he fell into the hands of
> robbers. They stripped him of his
> clothes, beat him and went away,
> leaving him half dead. A priest hap-
> pened to be going down the same
> road, and when he saw the man, he
> passed by on the other side. So too,
> a Levite, when he came to the place
> and saw him, passed by on the oth-
> er side. But a Samaritan, as he trav-
> eled, came where the man was; and
> when he saw him, he took pity on

him. He went to him and bandaged his wounds, pouring on oil and wine. Then he put the man on his own donkey, took him to an inn and took care of him. The next day he took out two silver coins and gave them to the innkeeper. 'Look after him,' he said, 'and when I return, I will reimburse you for any extra expense you may have.' "

(Luke 10:30–35)

Muggings have become a common part of modern urban life. They were not uncommon on the first-century "Way of Blood," the seventeen-mile road that plunged 3,300 feet from Jerusalem to Jericho. The old road traversed rugged, barren, lonely terrain and was favored by robber bands. In a day when all travel was hazardous, the Jericho road was especially so. The story the Lord tells is drawn from real life; its scenario is well known to his audience.

Jesus does not dwell on the mugging itself. Somewhere on that desolate road a lone traveler, almost certainly a Jew, is set upon by a band of robbers. He is not only robbed, but is also brutalized and left bloody, naked, and dying. Along the same road comes a priest.

Priests served in the temple on a rotational basis. Most of them lived outside of Jerusalem, and many lived in Jericho. The fact that this man is "going down" indicates that he is moving away from Jerusalem. Presumably, he has been involved in some form of temple service; almost certainly, he has engaged in temple worship. But suddenly he encounters a fellow Jew lying in a pool of blood, his life ebbing away. His reaction is instinctive. Carefully circling the situation, "he passed by on the other side."

The Lord doesn't tell us this man's rationale. But conjecture is not difficult. He is, after all, a priest. Contact with a dead body would be contaminating ceremonially (Lev. 21:1–4), and this victim is near death. The priest has already been away from home for a period of time, and the ritual of cleansing was costly and time consuming. At the very least, involvement would require a return to Jerusalem and the interruption of his plans. Besides, who could predict the difficulties and complications that involvement might bring?

I do not know, of course, that this is why the priest acted as he did. The Lord does not give his reasons. But all of us can understand fearing the contamination and complication

of contact with people in need. Involvement
with "problem people" often entangles us in
embarrassing, difficult, and even dangerous
situations. We may not feel good about
choosing the other side of the road, but we feel
a lot safer. Besides, others are better qualified.
"I'm a priest, not a paramedic."

The next man on the road is also a religious
figure, a Levite. Such men had important roles
in the service of the temple, although they did
not serve at the altar. This man's response
imitates that of the priest. His motives are not
given. Was it fear for his own safety (the robbers
may still be in the vicinity), a fear of defilement,
a fear of entanglement? For whatever reason,
he too "passed by on the other side."

We should not make the mistake of thinking
these are "bad" men. No, not bad, but busy.
For them and, too often, for me, people in need
are problems, interruptions, nuisances. They
intrude awkwardly on my privacy. They deflect
me from my duty. They distract me from my
responsibility. They keep me from my pleasures.
I agree that they need help, and I hope that
someone does help. But not me, not now, not
here. I have a different agenda.

By this time the Lord's audience is caught up in the parable. They love it when the clergy turn out to be the bad guys in the story. They can already guess who the hero will be—a "layman," an ordinary citizen, one of them. Certainly they could never expect the twist the tale takes with the words "but a Samaritan." We call this the story of "the good Samaritan," but to first-century Jews there was no such thing. This was as unthinkable as the good PLO member to the Zionist, the good IRA member to a North Irish Ulsterman, the good African National Congress follower to the Afrikaaner. The animosity between Jew and Samaritan was intense. The Jews believed that the Samaritans had defiled the temple, distorted the Torah, and degraded divine worship. Although he spoke two centuries later, Rabbi Shimon ben Jochai's words convey the attitude of first-century Jews toward their Samaritan neighbors: "They have no law, not even the remnants of a command, and are thus suspect and degenerate." For their part, the Samaritans returned the hostility in full measure.

The Lord is deliberately and carefully shocking his audience. His hero is a despised Samaritan, a man who does not pass by, whatever the pillars of Jewish religious society might do. However, it is not his nationality that sets him apart, but his *compassion.* He doesn't see anything the other two didn't, but he feels something they didn't. "He took pity on him." All of the normal hostility between Jew and Samaritan is swept away as he allows what he sees to affect his emotions and actions. Strikingly, the word translated here "pity" is used elsewhere in the Gospels only of the Lord Jesus. He, above all others, is the model of compassion.

But compassion is expressed in *care.* The Samaritan deals with the victim's immediate needs by bandaging his wounds and pouring on oil and wine. This man wouldn't be carrying a first-aid kit. Probably the bandages are provided by tearing up his own garments. Then he places the man on his own donkey and leads the animal down the hot, dusty road to an inn. This is an act that requires courage. After all, this is Jewish territory and a Samaritan transporting the Jewish victim of a mugging would be subject to all kinds of misunderstanding and misinterpretation. Imagine an Indian riding into Dodge City with a scalped cowboy draped over his horse! Once at the inn, he continues to look after the man. This is personal contact and care, not remote charity.

A third characteristic of the Samaritan is *commitment.* This victim is a total stranger, a man of another race and religion. He is stripped and penniless. Yet the Samaritan's compassion leads him further still, to assume responsibility for the man's future needs and debts: "When I return, I will reimburse you for any extra expense you may have." All this, with no plausible reason to believe there is any hope of recovering his expenditures. He is freely expressing undeserved and unexpected love to a person in need.

## The Practice of Love: The Great Challenge

> "Which of these three do you think was a neighbor to the man who fell into the hands of robbers?"
>
> The expert in the law replied, "The one who had mercy on him."
>
> Jesus told him, "Go and do likewise."
>
> (Luke 10:36–37)

With the Lord's question in verse 36 the story ends and the lesson begins. In a few short, well-chosen words, Jesus asks and answers not one question but several, each of which deserves our careful attention.

One question the Lord answers is the question that aroused the story, the theologian's question, *"Who is my neighbor?"* The answer is clear. My neighbor is not simply my fellow Jew, my fellow synagogue member, my fellow worshiper. My neighbor is that person who is in need, whose need I can see, whose need I can meet. My neighbor may be, on natural terms, my bitterest enemy. Were he well, that Jewish victim probably would have spat out the water offered by the Samaritan. My neighbor may be my religious opponent, a person with whom I have profound and important theological differences. My neighbor may be an unknown stranger who comes to me bloody and needy. Helping with his problems may be time-demanding and expensive, yet he may be unable to repay. And I meet him by chance (10:31—"happened"), not by appointment.

It misrepresents the Lord totally to suggest that He is saying that theological and religious matters are irrelevant "because we are all brothers." A brief reading of verses 8–16 of this chapter indicates just the opposite. But although we are not all spiritual brothers, we are all neighbors. Our need isn't to *define* who our neighbor is, but to *care for* him.

But there is an even more important question. Notice carefully Jesus' rephrasing of the issue in verse 36: "Which of these three do you think *became* [literal reading] a neighbor to the man who fell into the hands of robbers?" The Lord's concern isn't so much "who is my neighbor?" but "who became a neighbor?" The theologian can't bear to say "the Samaritan," so he answers, "the one who had mercy on him."

The central question is not "who is my neighbor?" but *"what is my duty?"* Again our need is not to define "neighbor" but to become the kind of person who cannot pass by on the other side. The three on the road all saw the same thing (10:31–33), but only one of the three felt compassion. This is the significant question: Am I concerned about calculating the limits of love or about caring for hurting people? The theologian is thinking about his responsibility; the Lord wants us to seize the opportunity. The theologian is thinking about himself; the Lord directs us to the sufferer.

The story is told of a young man named Bob who received a new car from his brother as a Christmas present. On Christmas Eve, when he came out of his office to drive it home, he noticed a street kid admiring the shiny car. "This yours, mister?" "Sure is. My brother gave it to me for Christmas." The boy was astonished. "You mean he just gave it to you, and it didn't cost you anything? Wow! Boy, I wish . . ." His voice trailed off. Bob finished the sentence in his mind. But what followed shook him. "I wish," the boy said, "that I could be a brother like that."

The young man was so astonished that he said impulsively, "Would you like a ride?" "Oh, yeah. That'd be great." So off they went, the boy's eyes sparkling with excitement. After a while he said, "Mister, would you mind stopping in front of my house?" "Ah, he wants to show off a little," Bob thought. "Will you stop where those two steps are?" Almost before the car had stopped, the boy was on his way into the house. A few moments later, he came back, and Bob saw to his amazement that he was carrying his little crippled brother. "There it is, John, just like I told you upstairs. His brother gave it to him, and it didn't cost him a cent. And someday

I'm going to get you one just like it, so we can go see all the things I keep telling you about."

Tears were flowing freely from Bob's eyes as he took that little boy and lifted him into his car to share a ride. For years after, he said the greatest gift he received that Christmas wasn't the car but the attitude of that young boy saying, "Boy, I wish I could be a brother like that!" That's what this parable should make us say: "I want to be a neighbor like that."

There is another question this parable asks and answers: *"What is love?"* Love is not a sentimental feeling. Rather it is sacrificial action. It means interrupting my schedule, expending my money, risking my reputation, ruining my property, even for a stranger, so that I can do what is best for him. Love is the compassion that feels, the care that involves, and the commitment that endures. Love originates in the giver of love, not the object of love. Love initiates, taking the first step in reaching out to those in need. Love pays the ultimate price—going to extraordinary lengths to help the hurting.

Although Christ does not dwell on the point, it is important to remember the connection between the two great commandments.

Love for God and love for one's neighbor are inextricably linked. In fact, love for people is the overflow of love for God. Ultimately, the reason why the priest and the Levite were able to pass by on the other side was that the love of God was not truly controlling them. Lack of compassion is a symptom of a deeper lack. Our willingness to become involved in the needs of others is the evidence of our experience of the love of God in our lives. "If anyone has material possessions and sees his brother in need but has no pity on him, how can the love of God be in him?" (1 John 3:17). As Martin Luther observed, "Faith alone justifies, yet faith is never alone. It is never without love; if love is lacking, neither is there faith, but mere hypocrisy." The Lord Jesus has given the world the right to challenge the reality of our faith by the reality of our love.

Hanging in the Lord's final challenge to the theologian, "Go and do likewise," is the question *What is my need*?" The Lord's challenge takes us full circle to the question of all of humanity: "What must I do to inherit eternal life?" If eternal life is won by doing and if eternal life is achieved by wholehearted love of God and Samaritan-like compassion, there is no hope for any of us. The theologian's great need lies in his relation to God. Jesus is the ultimate Samaritan, acting in costly love for His enemies. He did all the Samaritan did, and much more, by His death upon the cross. But His love is not only unique, it is also redemptive. The theologian needs more than an exhortation; he needs to acknowledge his need of a Savior.

The point of the Lord's parable is powerful. Loving my neighbor is not just good policy and socially appropriate behavior. Loving my neighbor is visible evidence of my relation to God. Gayle Erwin tells of engaging in a conversation at a Christian festival with two couples, one of whom was Buddhist. About halfway through the conversation, one of the Christians lit up a cigarette and apologized, saying that he was trying to give them up because he knew they hurt his testimony. The Buddhist woman immediately interjected, "We non-Christians, when one of our ranks becomes a Christian, don't watch them to see how well they live up to some self-imposed standard of piety. We watch them to see how they start treating people" (*The Jesus Style*).

Standards of behavior are not irrelevant. But meeting standards neither brings eternal life nor reveals its presence. The evidence of God's work in our lives is seen in more powerful ways. The Pharisees accused the Lord of subverting their standards, even of being a drunkard and a glutton. But they could never accuse Him of not loving people. Everything in His life revealed an unlimited love of neighbor, which was consistent with His perfect love of His Father. The model of the good Samaritan is overwhelmed by the model of the Good Shepherd. And His model must become the mandate of our lives.

# CHAPTER THREE

# THANKING MY SAVIOR

G. K. Chesterton was one of the remarkable individuals of the early twentieth century, a genius who combined the abilities of a novelist, critic, poet, popular theologian, and writer of detective stories. Toward the end of his life, he turned to the writing of his autobiography. As part of the process, he tried to state in a single sentence the most important lesson he had learned from life. After many false starts and wrong answers, he finally reached his conclusion. The most important thing he had learned, he claimed, was that the critical factor in life is whether you take things *for granted* or take them *with gratitude.*

Among the great ideas, that probably doesn't deserve to top the charts, but it does belong high on the list. Gratitude lubricates social interactions and its absence embitters the spirit and poisons relationships. Some people live as if they are entitled to life's good things and other people's kindnesses. That attitude quickly wears thin with those around them, and such people sentence themselves to loneliness. Unthankful people are almost always unhappy people.

But there is another dimension to the quality of gratitude. An attitude of overflowing thankfulness is one of the prime indicators of our relationship with God. When gratitude is lacking, grace has either not been received or not been understood. The state of our relationship with God is revealed clearly by our gratitude towards Him.

The Lord once told a story to show an ungrateful man how much his attitude exposed about his relationship with God. The story and its setting are found in Luke 7:36–50.

> Now one of the Pharisees invited Jesus to have dinner with him, so he went to the Pharisee's house and reclined at the table. When a woman who had lived a sinful life in that town learned that Jesus was eating at the Pharisee's house, she brought an alabaster jar of perfume, and as she stood behind him at his feet weeping, she began to wet his feet with her tears. Then she wiped them with her

hair, kissed them and poured perfume on them.

When the Pharisee who had invit-
ed him saw this, he said to himself,
"If this man were a prophet, he would
know who is touching him and what
kind of woman she is—that she is a
sinner."

Jesus answered him, "Simon, I
have something to tell you."

"Tell me, teacher," he said.

"Two men owed money to a certain moneylender. One owed him five
hundred denarii, and the other fifty.
Neither of them had the money to pay
him back, so he canceled the debts
of both. Now which of them will love
him more?"

Simon replied, "I suppose the one
who had the bigger debt canceled."

"You have judged correctly," Jesus
said.

Then he turned toward the woman and said to Simon, "Do you see
this woman? I came into your house.
You did not give me any water for
my feet, but she wet my feet with her

tears and wiped them with her hair. You did not give me a kiss, but this woman, from the time I entered, has not stopped kissing my feet. You did not put oil on my head, but she has poured perfume on my feet. Therefore, I tell you, her many sins have been forgiven—for she loved much. But he who has been forgiven little loves little."

Then Jesus said to her, "Your sins are forgiven."

The other guests began to say among themselves, "Who is this who even forgives sins?"

Jesus said to the woman, "Your faith has saved you; go in peace."

The Lord's parables are masterpieces when studied as isolated stories. But in their original context they have even more power and relevance. This episode occurs relatively early in Jesus' ministry in Galilee, but already He is experiencing the growing hostility of the Pharisees. The same hardness of heart that has led them to reject John the Baptist is leading them now to reject the Christ. While they ridicule John for his strict asceticism, they repudiate Jesus as "a glutton and a drunkard, a friend of tax collectors and 'sinners' " (Luke 7:34). Luke places this incident at Simon's house alongside that accusation to show that Jesus does indeed associate with sinners. However, the effect of that association is clear evidence that he is not "a glutton and a drunkard," but rather the Son of God.

## The Party: Expressing Love for Christ (7:36–39)

It is hard to discern the motive that led a Pharisee named Simon to invite Jesus home to share a meal. Jewish custom considered it meritorious to invite a traveling teacher for dinner, especially if he had preached in the local synagogue. Perhaps that was the reason. Or perhaps Simon was a celebrity hunter, infatuated with the new and the notorious. More probably, Simon wanted a closer look at this already infamous Jesus, and he was watching for a way to expose Him. Like many of his co-religionists, Simon was searching for a flaw in this man, who he was convinced was a religious fraud.

What is clear is that Simon treated Jesus with a callous disregard for the normal courtesies. The etiquette of hospitality is well-established in most cultures. In ancient Palestine this included such things as the kiss of greeting and making provision for the washing of a guest's feet (7:44–46). But these niceties were not part of Simon's greeting. Were I to visit your home on a cold winter's night, and you didn't offer to take my coat or welcome me in or show me where to sit, I would soon feel very ill at ease. Was Simon's behavior a studied insult, a deliberate downgrading of the guest of honor, so that he could show his other guests what he thought of this Jesus? Or was it cold formality?—that is, Simon might have acted correctly but carefully, doing no more than was strictly necessary. We cannot be certain, but we can be sure that the mood at the table was not one of relaxed and casual warmth. The atmosphere was stiff, the tone formal, the feeling tense.

But Jesus was there. The fact that He was a friend of sinners did not mean that He was unwilling to be a friend of the respectable and self-righteous. They also needed the gospel He had come to bring.

Jewish dinner parties during the first century were not like ours. While the guests were reclining at the table, needy people were permitted to come to take the leftovers as they became available. In addition, those who were curious were allowed to sit against the wall and observe the proceedings. So it was no surprise when an uninvited woman entered the room. But suddenly, after the shock of recognition, came the gasp of surprise. Not just a woman, but *this* woman! For she was notorious throughout the town for her immoral way of life. This woman and this event should not be confused with Mary of Bethany and the anointing of Jesus described in John 12:1–8. There are obvious similarities, but the differences are too important to ignore. This event occurs in Galilee; the other, in Bethany. This occurs early in the Lord's public ministry; the other, towards the end. This woman is a public sinner; Mary of Bethany, a respected member of society. This is not the kind of woman who normally would ever set foot in the house of a man like Simon! What is this sinner doing here? The way she is treated shows that she is an infamous woman—perhaps an adulteress or even a prostitute. Clearly, something dramatic is about to happen.

If her presence isn't shocking enough, her behavior exceeds all the boundaries of propriety. Her visit isn't the whim of a moment, for she has come prepared. She is carrying "an alabaster jar of perfume," an expensive material used for the embalming of a body or the anointing of a king. Where she had previously met the Lord Jesus we do not know. What He had done for her spiritual need we can only guess. Now she approaches Him, obviously intending to anoint His feet as an act of love and devotion. But suddenly, as she stands behind the reclining Jesus, her emotions get the better of her. Overcome by love, she begins to weep, and her tears shower down upon the Lord's feet. Impulsively, she undoes her hair, wipes His feet with it, smothers them with kisses, then breaks her vase and pours the perfume upon them.

The room falls silent as the guests sit stunned. The whole series of events is unthinkable. This is a woman—and an unclean, sinful woman, at that, whose very touch is contaminating! What right does she have to intrude on men's table fellowship? The Talmud says that a woman can be divorced for unbinding her hair in the presence of other men. That is bad enough, but to use it to wipe a man's feet! . . . No words are adequate to condemn such behavior. If an obvious streetwalker were to walk into the midst of a church service, rush to the platform weeping and throw herself at the preacher's feet in an avalanche of tears, how would you respond?

Simon can hardly believe his eyes. He is shocked by the woman's actions and emotions, which are excessive even for such a person. But he is even more shocked by Jesus' response. Christ doesn't jump to His feet in indignation, condemn the woman, and send her away. In fact, Jesus not only doesn't discourage this woman, He accepts and even encourages her! How could He be a man of God, possessing spiritual insight? "If this man were a prophet, he would know who is touching him and what kind of woman she is—that she is a sinner," Simon concludes.

Simon's unspoken thoughts probably revolve around three things. First, he has contempt for the woman. She is an untouchable, unacceptable sinner, whose well-known sins have made her an outcast. All good people shun such a person. "It is bad enough that she's in my house, but for her to behave like this is outrageous." Second, he has a complaint about Jesus. He knew that something about Jesus made it difficult to see Him as merely another man. He seemed almost to be a prophet, or perhaps more. But how could He be a prophet and condone such behavior? Surely, a man in touch with God would have more insight and discernment than Jesus has displayed. Everything in Simon's experience has told him that good people protect their goodness by avoiding sinful people. Third, he has confidence in himself. Pushed to the wall, Simon would admit that he was a sinner, but not a sinner like this woman. Contact with him wasn't defiling. He was qualitatively different from a prostitute. He might be a little sinner, but she was a great sinner, fundamentally different from him. If Jesus couldn't see that, then Jesus couldn't truly be a prophet.

Jesus reads Simon's thoughts like an open book. Simon complains that Jesus doesn't know "who is touching him." In fact, He knows not only who and what kind of person the woman is, but exactly who and what kind of person Simon is. And so He tells Simon a story that both explains the woman's attitude and exposes Simon's.

## The Parable: Understanding Love for Jesus (7:40–43)

The Lord's story is short and simple. Two men are indebted to the same moneylender. One man owes the equivalent of five hundred days' wages (a denarius was what a working man would receive per day), while the other owes fifty days' wages. But both are equally impoverished. It should be observed that, in the most important sense, these men are equal. When you have no resources, the question of who has the greater debt is purely academic. In a parallel sense, if none of us can pay the debt of sin, it does little good to determine that someone else is a greater sinner. Spiritual bankruptcy, like financial bankruptcy, is a great equalizer.

But this moneylender, for no apparent reason, "canceled the debts of both." This translation, although accurate, obscures an important term used by Luke. More precisely, we are told that "he graciously forgave the debts." The Savior's word (*charizomai*) has as its base the great biblical word *grace* (*charis*).

It is used in pre-Christian Greek to mean such things as "to give cheerfully," "to give freely." The basic idea is "to make a gift," and here it means that "he made a gift of what they owed" and so "forgave" their debts. In other words, the lender forgave them by assuming their debts himself. He didn't explain, excuse, or extend the debts; he forgave them and ended them. It was an act of grace, because he did not require the men to work off even a portion of what they owed. It was an act of freedom, because he did not merely extend the payment period. Instead he forgave the debtors and let them go. This is the very essence of grace.

But that simple act does not stand alone. The Lord ends His story with a question: "Which of them will love him more?" The implications of this simple question are important. There is a link between love and forgiveness. *Forgiveness precedes love*. The forgiven person will love the forgiver, because he has been forgiven. In fact, there will be a direct correlation between our perception of forgiveness and our feeling of love. Where there is forgiveness there will inevitably be love. Love is a response to pure grace, aroused by gratitude. It is also true that *gratitude expresses love*. Love is shown to the forgiver. "Who will love *him* more?" The implication is important. If this woman shows love to Jesus, it is because Jesus is her forgiver. He is implicitly claiming to be God. But the chain of response is clear: forgiveness arouses love, which is expressed by gratitude. And both love and gratitude are shown to the forgiver.

The response of Simon to the Lord's question seems rather reluctant: "I suppose the one who had the bigger debt canceled" (more precisely, "The one he forgave most"). Apparently he is beginning to feel the pressure build, as Jesus' point becomes more obvious. He reluctantly states the obvious conclusion. But the Lord does not allow him to view this as merely an interesting story. He agrees with Simon's answer, and then specifically addresses himself first to Simon and then to the woman.

## The Pardon: Diagnosing Our Love for Jesus (7:44–50)

From childhood, we are taught not to comment on a host's shortcomings. We eat what we are served and graciously refrain from critical statements. We give compliments; we do not express complaints. Undoubtedly, the Lord would have politely overlooked the shortcomings of Simon's hospitality, had He not had a far more important lesson to teach. Simon's lack of etiquette was trivial compared with his spiritual need. Jesus wasn't evaluating the Pharisee's skill as a host so much as He was diagnosing his condition before God.

The contrast between Simon and the woman is stark. For whatever reason, Simon had done the least possible for Jesus. His feet had remained unwashed, His cheeks unkissed, His hair unanointed. The woman's extravagance, on the other hand, had known no bounds. She had thrown convention and propriety to the winds to lavish her love and gratitude upon Jesus. Her hair had been the towel for His feet; her kisses had covered them; her perfume had been their ointment.

"Do you see this woman?" Jesus asks. In fact, Simon doesn't. He sees not a woman but a sinner. He has frozen her in her past. But Jesus sees not a sinner but a worshiper. He sees her present, not her past—her forgiveness, not her failure. In verse 47 we are told the secret of the transformation: "Therefore, I tell you, her many sins have been forgiven—for she loved much. But he who has been forgiven little loves little." The translation of this verse is not without its problems, but its message is clear. The parable clearly indicates that forgiveness produces love, not vice versa. This woman is not forgiven because she loves. Rather, her love is the evidence that she already has been forgiven. Two things are obvious about her: her past sin and her present love for Jesus. The Lord now makes clear that great love has followed great sin because this woman has experienced great forgiveness. The missing link in the chain of her life that explains her behavior is the Lord's forgiveness of her.

It should be observed that it is *love shown to Jesus that is the evidence of forgiveness*. The responses of Simon and the woman to Jesus himself are the indicators of whether they have been forgiven much or little. He is the Forgiver, because He is God. This means that the presence or absence of love for Jesus Christ in me is directly related to my understanding and experience of forgiveness. This is a challenge to careful self-examination, and it raises a probing question: "If gratitude is a sign of forgiveness, of what is lack of gratitude a sign?" If I show a lack of love for Christ, what does that say about my relation to God? Simon did not love the Lord, because he did not know the Lord. An unforgiven person can treat Jesus Christ with polite formality; a forgiven person cannot.

The Lord's words force another question. Is there such a thing as someone who is "forgiven little?" Undeniably, Simon felt that he was a "little sinner," especially in comparison with this woman. But that is only true if sins of the spirit are less important than sins of the flesh. The Scripture is emphatic that they are not. We label the adulterer and the thief as big sinners. But God hates pride, self-righteousness, and criticism with all the vehemence of His holy nature. John Owen observed that "he who has slight thoughts of sin never has great thoughts of God." That was precisely Simon's problem. Because he trivialized his sin, he misunderstood what God's forgiveness meant. We are not forgiven more or less; we are forgiven all or nothing. Simon was not different from this woman qualitatively. Like her, he was spiritually bankrupt, in need of a Savior to cancel his debt. His greatest need was to realize the magnitude of his need for forgiveness.

Having probed the heart of Simon, the Lord turned to the woman. He spoke for her sake, but also for the sake of others standing by. He wanted there to be no doubt of the spiritual realities involved.

## Jesus and the Woman (7:48–50)

In the early months of 1989, the Muslim world arose in fury over a novel which they claimed demeaned the prophet Mohammed. People were killed in riots against *The Satanic Verses*, and the Ayatollah Khomeini ordered zealous Muslims to kill the author, Salman Rushdie. Rushdie responded by expressing his regret that his book had caused distress to sincere followers of Islam. To which Khomeini responded, "Even if Salman Rushdie repents and becomes the most pious man of all time, it is incumbent on every Muslim to employ everything he has, his life and wealth, to send him to hell."

To some people, forgiveness is an impossibility and sin is an indelible stain. To many more in our morally confused world, forgiveness is a formality, the obvious response of a loving God to sin. Few people really believe the latter when put to the test, however. If someone's daughter is raped or a mass murder is committed, then we cry out for justice and even vengeance. But when we think about *our* sins, we comfort ourselves, concluding that they aren't really a major problem to God and that even if they are distasteful to Him, He is kind enough to overlook them. A society that discounts sin inevitably cheapens forgiveness.

Simon apparently viewed this woman much as Khomeini viewed Rushdie, as being irremediably guilty. The most she could hope for was a long period of moral probation. And I suspect that she had held the same view of herself. But Jesus did not. Unequivocally He declares, "Your sins are forgiven." He is saying much more than, "In my opinion you are forgiven." The absoluteness of His word of forgiveness is breathtaking. I can forgive someone's sins against me personally, but not their "sins" in general, and in total. That is God's prerogative, since all sin is directed against Him (Ps. 51:4). By declaring that this woman has been forgiven, Jesus is taking the place of God himself, and His hearers recognize the implications: "Who is this who even forgives sins?" (Compare Luke 5:21.) The fact is that Jesus knows exactly who He is—the Son of God sent by the Father to pronounce forgiveness.

But Jesus does not forgive sin by trivializing it. Although the basis of her forgiveness is not stated here, it is in the rest of the New Testament. This woman is not forgiven because of her repentance or faith, but because of the atoning death of Christ. Just as the moneylender in the parable forgave those indebted to him by, in effect, paying their debts himself, the Lord Jesus will pay the spiritual debt of this woman by dying for her on the cross. "In him we have redemption through his blood, the forgiveness of sins . . ." (Eph. 1:7). This is not a cheap forgiveness. The words that the Lord speaks mean for Him nothing less than the anguish of crucifixion and separation from His heavenly Father. *Forgiveness is costly.*

Jesus is the forgiver because He is the sin-bearer. His forgiveness means a paying for and letting go by God of our guilt and penalty. The Greek word for forgiveness in verse 48 is different from that used in verse 42. The word in the earlier verse means "to forgive by making a gift." The debt is paid. The word in verse 48 means "to release, let go, cancel." Our sins are finally and completely gone, totally obliterated by the work of Christ. Not a trace of them remains before a holy God. *Forgiveness is final.* There is no such thing as partial or temporary forgiveness. This woman, and every forgiven sinner, stands absolutely clean before God. *Forgiveness is also free.* Based on Christ's work, it is received by faith. "Your faith has saved you . . ." (7:50). The Lord does not impose preconditions before we qualify. Trust in Christ, reliance upon Him, brings salvation to a prostitute, no matter how outrageous this may seem to a self-righteous Pharisee. This has nothing to do with the virtue of faith; it has everything to do with the value of Christ's blood. *And forgiveness is public.* It is not simply a private transaction between the soul and God. The Lord publicly associates himself with this forgiven woman. Simon may be embarrassed by her, but the sinless, holy Son of God is not. He accepts her touch and appreciates her worship.

The results of the Lord's words are revolutionary for this woman. Because of Jesus, she has found *a new freedom.* She has acted as if He is the only one in the room. The sneers of the respectable and the insults of the religious cannot control her. As James Denney observes about her behavior: "What an extraordinary demonstration! We are tempted to say, 'Was it

hysterics, the weakness of a breaking wave?'
No, it was not hysterics, it was regeneration. It
was the new birth of faith and hope and love,
evoked and welcomed by Jesus; it was the
passionate experience of a sinner's relation to
God" (*The Christian Doctrine of Reconciliation*).
For the first time in her life, a man has made her
feel clean instead of dirty. For the first time in
her life, she can walk into the Pharisee's house
and say, no matter what anyone else may say,
"That Man has set me free from what I was."

Forgiveness has also meant for her *a new
love.* She had used her body to traffic in the
act of love, yet perhaps her heart had known
nothing of the warmth of true love. But with
forgiveness came an inward cleansing, and
springs of pure emotion poured forth love
and gratitude. Perhaps Simon could be coldly
correct with Jesus, but how could she?

Finally, forgiveness had become the entrance
into *a new peace.* "Your faith has saved you; go
in peace." This was, above all, peace with God
and therefore peace within herself. Listen again
to James Denney:

> Apparently she was a sinner in the
> city, one of that unhappy class who

walk the streets and live by sin. There
are none in the world more friendless, none from whom the passers-by
more instinctively turn aside, none
whom ordinary society would be so
determined not to receive. . . . Jesus
did not shrink from the sinful woman: He received her. He took her part
against the Pharisee. . . . And as she
went, she knew that friendless as she
had been before she had now a friend
with God; it is not too much to say,
she knew that God Himself was her
friend.

(*The Christian Doctrine of Reconciliation*)

This woman went out a very different woman
than she had come in. The audience may
have murmured at the Lord's forgiveness, but
neither she nor the Lord paid any attention. He
declared it, and she grasped it.

The story and the parable force us to
profound self-examination. Their meaning
cannot be clearer: gratitude and love for Jesus
are the evidence of forgiveness. Most of us do
not have this woman's sordid history. But the
real question is whether or not we have her

singing heart. Not to love is not to have grasped forgiveness. If the spring doesn't bubble, the problem may lie at its source. Or if we are truly forgiven but only mildly grateful, that is a sure sign that we have somehow polluted the bubbling spring of the Spirit. Only a return to the cross will free us to see again the enormity of our sin and the cost of our forgiveness. But then we must determine to break the alabaster vase, pour it out in love on our Lord, and fill the room with the fragrance of our grateful worship.

What is this parable in this context designed to tell us? Simply that thanking our Savior is the natural response to having been forgiven by our Savior, and that our love for the Lord Jesus demonstrated in public thankfulness reveals our forgiveness by Him. There are no little sinners; there is no little forgiveness. So properly there can be no little love and no little gratitude.

Go ahead. Break the vase! Pour it out! He's worth it.

# CHAPTER FOUR

# FORGIVING MY BROTHER

One of my favorite stories concerns a man who was bitten by a dog, which was later discovered to be rabid. The man was rushed to the hospital where tests revealed that he had, in fact, contracted rabies. At the time, medical science had no solution for this problem, and his doctor faced the difficult task of informing him that his condition was incurable and terminal. "Sir, we will do all we can to make you comfortable. But I cannot give you false hope. There is nothing we can really do. My best advice is that you put your affairs in order as soon as possible." The dying man sank back on his bed in shock, but finally rallied enough strength to ask for a pen and some paper. He then set to work with great energy. An hour later, when the doctor returned, the man was still writing vigorously. "I'm glad to see that you're working on your will." "This ain't no will, Doc. This is a list of people I'm going to bite before I die."

Many of us live and die with that kind of list, written in our minds, if not on paper. It is a list of people whom we believe have wronged, hurt, misused, misjudged, or mistreated us. Sometimes there are no specific names—just a bitterness about life and people that poisons the spirit and can erupt into terrible acts of violence. The results can be horrific—a man angry at women guns down innocent college co-eds; a man boards a plane to shoot the man who fired him the day before, then murders the pilot and the co-pilot, plunging all aboard to a fiery death; terrorists, bearing deep hatreds and a desire for revenge, maim, kill, and destroy indiscriminately.

But the results are often less spectacular—a marriage destroyed, a family divided, a church split, a friendship ruined, a business partnership devastated. At the root of all these greater and lesser tragedies is an unforgiving spirit, a refusal to let go a wrong suffered that locks an individual into a prison of his own making, where resentment, bitterness, and anger become one's constant companions.

It is easy to proclaim the virtue of forgiveness. But reality is another matter. C. S. Lewis put it so well: "Forgiveness is a beautiful word, until you have something to forgive." Something powerful within us clings to wrongs suffered and longs to strike back at our tormentors. Precisely because this desire is so strong, the Lord Jesus dealt with the need to forgive on numerous occasions. Obviously He considered it to be one of life's crucial issues, and His entire life was both a lesson about forgiveness and a provision for it. Perhaps His most important message about the subject was given in the form of a parable, the story of the unforgiving servant found in Matthew 18:21–35.

> Then Peter came to Jesus and asked, "Lord, how many times shall I forgive my brother when he sins against me? Up to seven times?"
>
> Jesus answered, "I tell you, not seven times, but seventy-seven times.
>
> "Therefore, the kingdom of heaven is like a king who wanted to settle accounts with his servants. As he began the settlement, a man who owed him ten thousand talents was brought to him. Since he was not able to pay, the master ordered that he and his wife

and his children and all that he had be sold to repay the debt.

"The servant fell on his knees before him. 'Be patient with me,' he begged, 'and I will pay back everything.' The servant's master took pity on him, canceled the debt and let him go.

"But when that servant went out, he found one of his fellow servants who owed him a hundred denarii. He grabbed him and began to choke him. 'Pay back what you owe me!' he demanded.

"His fellow servant fell to his knees and begged him, 'Be patient with me, and I will pay you back.'

"But he refused. Instead, he went off and had the man thrown into prison until he could pay the debt. When the other servants saw what had happened, they were greatly distressed and went and told their master everything that had happened.

"Then the master called the servant in. 'You wicked servant,' he said, 'I canceled all that debt of yours because you begged me to. Shouldn't you have had mercy on your fellow servant just as I had on you?' In anger his master turned him over to the jailers to be tortured, until he should pay back all he owed.

"This is how my heavenly Father will treat each of you unless you forgive your brother from your heart."

Matthew arranged his gospel around five great teaching discourses of the Savior. Matthew 18 is the fourth of those and it concerns the subject of relationships among His kingdom people. The Lord speaks first about the need for being childlike and having humility (18:1–14), but then reminds His followers in verses 15–20 that the kingdom requires that they suffer the consequences of their wrong choices, one of which is exclusion from fellowship. Yet the goal is always to win the brother, to restore sinful people.

## The Problem of Forgiveness: Seventy Times Seven

I have a great love for Peter. He continually blurts out the questions I would love to have asked, as he blunders his way toward spiritual understanding. As the Lord talks about reproving a brother who has sinned, Peter's mind latches upon the statement, "If he listens to you, you have won your brother over" (18:15b). As he mulls that over, it becomes obvious to him that this requires not only the sinning brother's response, but also the confronting brother's forgiveness. Relationships are recaptured only when brothers forgive. But Peter is hardheaded enough to know that forgiveness is hard work. Furthermore, he has been taught by the rabbis that forgiveness is essential, but limited. "You must forgive three times," they said. "But the fourth time you must not forgive." Knowing something of his Master, he gropes for a new standard: "Lord, how many times shall I forgive my brother when he sins against me? Up to seven times?"

Give Peter credit. He has doubled the rabbis and added one. But to understand the parable we need to reflect carefully upon the question. First, Peter is asking about a brother, a fellow believer. The Lord has posed the issue, "If your brother sins . . ." This is not to suggest that forgiveness is limited to certain relationships; it is to say that it must be practiced with particular urgency within the kingdom community.

Second, Peter is asking about present relationships. It is my present responsibility, and not final judgment, that is in view. This is an important perspective to bring to the parable. Third and most important, Peter is asking about forgiveness. It is important to think clearly at this point. Forgiveness is not excusing other people when you come to "understand" their actions. Forgiveness deals with sin, and if behavior can be excused, it needs to be accepted, not forgiven. Nor is forgiveness "forgetting," allowing something to slip out of our minds. When God "forgets" our sins, they do not slip out of His omniscience. To say that He does not remember them *against us* is not the same as to say that He does not remember them. Something that can be forgotten is trivial; things that truly need forgiveness are not. And forgiveness is not ignoring, avoiding, or being indifferent to a person who has harmed us, a state of controlled politeness. President Eisenhower once described his personal policy in this way:

> I make it a practice to avoid hating anyone. If someone has been guilty of despicable actions, especially

towards me, I try to forget him. I used
to follow a practice—somewhat con-
trived I admit—to write the man's
name on a scrap of paper, drop it into
my bottom drawer and say to myself,
"That finishes the incident, and as far
as I'm concerned, that person." That
drawer became over the years a sort
of private wastebasket for crumpled
up spite and discarded personalities.
Besides, it seemed to be effective
and helped me avoid harboring useless black feelings.

Eisenhower may have been a great general
and an effective president, but his practice
bears no resemblance to biblical forgiveness.
Christians should not fill wastebaskets with
discarded people. Yet, in reality, they often do,
and the fragile nature of relationships in many
families and churches indicates that this is so.
If we are to come to grips with forgiveness,
there are three things that we must realize.
First, forgiveness deals with real sin, with
the inexcusable, the unforgettable, and
the unacceptable. As G. K. Chesterton
wrote, "Forgiveness means pardoning the

unpardonable or it is not forgiveness at all."
Second, forgiveness means erasing the act,
letting go of the wrong. That is the precise
meaning of the Greek word used in Matthew
18:21. There should be letting go of the
desire to get revenge, a release of the entire
situation to the Lord. This is not the same as
reconciliation. Reconciliation is the rebuilding
of a trusting relationship and takes time.
Forgiveness is the prerequisite for reconciliation.
Forgiveness is always within my power, through
the enabling of the Spirit. Reconciliation is not,
much as I might desire it. Third, forgiveness is
granted, not earned. I choose to forgive. I am
not to wait until I am no longer hurt by what was
done. Forgiveness is a servant of the will, not a
prisoner of the emotions. It is not easy: it may in
fact be the hardest thing we ever do. But there
is no option. Forgiveness is the will of God.
Peter, I'm sure, was somewhat overwhelmed
by the thought of forgiving seven times. The
Lord's reply must have stunned him: "I tell you,
not seven times, but seventy-seven times." That
translation is itself surprising to those familiar
with the King James "seventy times seven."
Why the difference? There is an ambiguity
in the Greek text that reads simply "seventy,

seven." This could mean, depending on context, either "seventy plus seven" or "seventy times seven." There is a fascinating parallel here to the song of Lamech in Genesis 4:23–24. Lamech's is a shout of revenge and retaliation: "I have killed a man for wounding me, a young man for injuring me. If Cain is avenged seven times, then Lamech seventy-seven times." That is the natural human tendency—to get revenge with interest. "Don't get mad, get even." But "even" isn't really enough. "I'm going to make you pay. You'll never do that again." There's a lot of Dirty Harry in each of us, daring someone to "go ahead, make my day."

The way of the Savior is entirely different. Whether it is seventy-seven times or seventy times seven the call is to an unlimited response. The Lord is asking us not to count how often we forgive at all. This is a supernatural response, possible only by God's grace within us. The natural man craves revenge. The disciple of the Lord is to overflow with forgiveness. Why that is so is the point of the parable of the unforgiving servant, which comes next in His discourse.

## The Parable of Forgiveness:
## The Unmerciful Servant

The Lord's story takes us into the affairs of state of a great king. As we think of him we are to think of God. The leader of a great empire, this king has a multitude of ministers and bureaucrats answerable to him, men charged with the administration of his realm. One such individual owes the king "ten thousand talents." Even in our day of incredible salaries paid to athletes and entertainers, this is an enormous sum. A talent was a weight of money equal to six thousand denarii. Since a working man received one denarius a day, one talent was the equivalent of twenty years' wages, conservatively a quarter of a million dollars in today's terms. Here is a man who owes ten thousand of these, a debt of over two billion dollars! Here is a man who has been looting the king's treasury on a scale that would be envied by a Ferdinand Marcos!

But when accounting day comes, the servant is unable to pay the king back. Not only is he hopelessly and criminally in debt, he is absolutely bankrupt. His debt means slavery, not only for him but for all of his family. Why does the Lord use such astronomical figures?

He is trying to remind us of our debt before a holy God. We tend to see sin as a little thing. After all, we all do it. But sin is no small matter to an absolutely righteous and perfect God. Sin places me in a position of spiritual bankruptcy, with an obligation I could not discharge, were I given all eternity to do it.

Confronted by the consequences of his failure, this man can only plead for time. Even here he is blind to his plight. "Be patient with me, and I will pay back everything." He apparently has not grasped the truth about his problem. But the king responds in an amazing way: He "took pity on him, canceled the debt and let him go." It is important to recognize what the king does and why. The motive is compassion. It is the character of the king, not the character of the servant, that produces the release from debt. *The reason for forgiveness is found in the forgiver, not the forgiven.* It is an act of grace. This is the great truth about our forgiveness through Christ. God, being who He is, chooses to forgive us in grace. And that is the model of all forgiveness. The nature of forgiveness is release from debt by the payment of a price. The king, in effect, turns the debt into a gift. The money is his, and he gives up the right to it. *The forgiver pays what the forgiven owes.* Only the king can forgive the debt, and he forgives it by paying it himself. On a far more important level, this is the message of the gospel. The debt sinners owe to a holy God is paid for by the debt-holder himself, God the Son, through His death on the cross.

The way in which this parable will become reality through the Lord's death is, of course, hidden from Peter as he listens to it. But as he hears the response of the servant to this incredible act of forgiveness, the point of the story becomes clear. The free and forgiven man has no sooner left the palace than he meets a fellow servant who owes him money. This man owes one hundred denarii, a considerable sum of perhaps $3,000. More importantly, it is exactly one-six hundred thousandth of what he has just been forgiven! The amount is trivial in light of what he owed, and besides, he doesn't need the money! He has been forgiven!

But his response is harsh and severe. "He grabbed him and began to choke him. 'Pay back what you owe me!' " The debtor's response is revealing. He does exactly what this servant had done before the king. He falls to his knees begging, "Be patient with me, and I will pay you back." It is important to think carefully about this picture. The first servant has a legal right to demand repayment and inflict judgment on the debtor. The second man is in the wrong. He has failed to pay his debts, and the law agreed in the culture of the day that such a man could be punished and thrown into jail. This reminds us that the opposite of forgiveness is punishment. But although he has a legal right to demand payment, he has no moral right. It is impossible to receive forgiveness gratefully from one and to refuse it vengefully to another. When I choose to receive forgiveness, I obligate myself to practice forgiveness.

The inconsistency of the servant's actions becomes a scandal in the king's household. Burdened by the unfairness of it all, others in the king's retinue feel compelled to tell the king. You don't have to be royalty to recognize how a forgiven person ought to act. And the king's response is clear. His anger is aroused by the man's actions. After a biting condemnation, "his master turned him over to the jailers to be tortured, until he should pay back all he owed." Torture was not a biblical form of punishment, but the Lord's words describe common practice in a land ruled by Herod and the Romans.

Justification for torture was built on the idea
that the man had hidden his borrowed funds
and would reveal them under duress.

Is the Lord suggesting that God the Father is
a sadist? Is He teaching that forgiven believers
might be unforgiven later and punished
eternally? It is dangerous to read the parables
as if every detail had theological significance.
But if there is a point being made here, it deals
with the present, not the eternal, consequences
of an unforgiving spirit. There is a torment, a
torture that is more real than physical pain. I
recall saying to a woman, after her long recital
of her husband's failures and shortcomings, "It
seems to me that you choose either to forgive
or to end your marriage." "I'd rather be angry,"
she shouted, stamping out of the office and
soon after into a divorce court. I can also think
of the agony of a young man who would not let
go of his wife's indiscretion prior to marriage.
His compulsion to retell the story and expose
every nook and cranny of the episode not
only poisoned their marriage and every other
relationship they had, it locked him in a torture
chamber of his own making that threatened his
emotional and mental stability. I have sat with a
man whose interpretation of a fellow Christian's

questionable dealings with him in business had twisted the way he viewed every other Christian and even God himself. The torture chamber of an unforgiving spirit is all too real and, ironically, has as its chief victim the person so sure of his moral and legal rectitude. As S. I. McMillen observed in *None of These Diseases*, "The moment I start hating a man I become his slave. He even controls my thoughts. I can't escape his tyrannical grasp on my mind. When the waiter serves me steak it might as well be stale bread and water. The man I hate will not permit me to enjoy it."

## The Principles of Forgiveness: The Kingdom Lifestyle

The Lord has no intention of allowing us to dismiss this story as an entertaining but irrelevant tale. "This is how my heavenly Father will treat each of you unless you forgive your brother from your heart." He is speaking to disciples, and His words remind us that this basic teaching on forgiveness is standard operating procedure, applicable to every kingdom citizen. There are at least three major truths that we must consider.

*First, the source of forgiveness is God's forgiveness.* The parable clearly indicates that we need to understand the extent of our debt before a righteous and holy God. Like the servant, we are faced with a burden that is beyond our capacity, a mountain of sin that we cannot budge, never mind remove. Until we see ourselves as truly and deeply sinful, we will see nothing else clearly. We also need to understand the cost of forgiveness. I have been the recipient of people's generosity that has left me speechless. I realize that their love has been costly, and I am overwhelmed by the cost. It cost the king two to three billion dollars to forgive his sinful servant. How can we comprehend that kind of forgiveness? But it cost God the Father His own Son to forgive my sins. It cost the Lord Jesus Calvary to bring me forgiveness. Everything else flows from this: I was hopelessly in debt; I was fully, freely, and finally forgiven through the sacrificial death of the Lord Jesus in the grace of God. The reason lies totally in the forgiver. I do not and cannot deserve forgiveness, but I can enjoy it because God is the kind of God He is.

*Second, the refusal to forgive is costly.* Often we are overwhelmed by the cost of forgiveness.

"If you only knew what that person did to me," you might say. I have no desire to minimize the extent of the evil that was done or the difficulty of letting it go. Nor am I suggesting that reconciliation is always possible, especially when that other person refuses to accept responsibility or acknowledge wrongdoing. But I do insist that you recall what your sin did to the Son of God and what it cost Him to declare you forgiven. As a consequence, you have a responsibility to let go of that wrong done to you. First, let it go to the Lord. Release that other person from your desire to retaliate. This is not a once-for-all act but a choice that needs to be remade continually. Then trust God for the wisdom and strength to face what the future may hold.

But listen carefully to the Lord. To accept God's forgiveness and to refuse to forgive another is not just unfortunate, it is *wicked*. That is startling, but the king's words are, "you wicked servant." Then, as we have seen, to refuse to forgive is *enslaving*. The jail and the torturers are real. When Robert E. Lee came through her area after the Civil War, a woman in Virginia showed him on her property a tree damaged by Yankee artillery. Lee's advice was straightforward: "Cut it down, dear lady, and forget it." To nurture the damaged trees of wrongs done to us is to be a prisoner of the past. To refuse to forgive is also *destructive.* The picture of the unforgiving servant grabbing his debtor around the neck to choke him is eloquent. I have seen that spirit choke the life out of a marriage or out of a family relationship or a friendship. Our society is littered with the corpses of choked relationships, but the pattern is most often a murder-suicide in which both parties are destroyed.

A missionary couple returned from years of serving in the Far East only to find that financial difficulties forced them to live in a rough neighborhood. They were just settling in when their son was brutally attacked by a local gang. The attack, with a nail-studded rope, left their son virtually blind and requiring extensive cosmetic surgery. The perpetrators were found, tried, and sentenced. The brutality of the attack had inflamed public opinion, so the case was well covered. Despite the media's best efforts, the family refused to be drawn into opportunities to attack those guilty of such senseless brutality. When the trial was all over, reporters asked for an explanation of the parents' behavior. The mother expressed it simply: "If necessary, we can live with a physical handicap. But we can't live with a bitter spirit." Wise words, well learned in the Savior's school of forgiveness.

A final lesson of the parable is that *the secret of forgiveness is grace*. God's grace does not free us from responsibility; on the contrary, it creates obligation. Grace received means grace must be displayed. "Shouldn't you have had mercy on your fellow servant just as I had on you?" The phrase translated "shouldn't you" is quite literally "wasn't it necessary?" There is nothing optional about forgiveness: it is part of the logic of Calvary. "Be kind and compassionate to one another, forgiving each other, just as in Christ God forgave you" (Eph. 4:32). The duty to forgive is not grounded in society's needs or our common humanity. It is grounded in Calvary. What the Lord did shows what we must do.

This means that forgiveness is a choice made because of the will of God. But it is also a possibility available because of the power of God within us. Forgiveness is the great evidence that we have become new creatures in Christ and that the Spirit of Christ lives within us. During World War II Corrie ten Boom was confined in the concentration camp at Ravensbruck for her part in sheltering Jews from their Nazi oppressors. Her father died in another camp, and in the dehumanizing conditions of Ravensbruck she was not only humiliated and degraded, but she watched the life of her sister Betsy ebb away. Yet God's grace was real in the midst of all the suffering, and after the war she went to Germany to preach God's forgiveness.

Following one service, a man came forward whom she recognized immediately. One of the worst experiences in camp had been the delousing showers where the women were ogled and taunted by leering guards. This man was one of those S. S. guards, a man who had been one of the cruelest, especially to her sister. Now he stood in front of her, with his hand outstretched. "*Ja fraulein*, it is wonderful that Jesus forgives all our sins, just as you say." Corrie froze as all the memories flooded back, but the man carried on. "You mentioned Ravensbruck. I was a guard there, but since then I have become a Christian. I know that God has forgiven me, but I would like to hear it from you as well. *Fraulein*, will you forgive me?"

Corrie stood there paralyzed. She couldn't forgive. Betsy had died there; she had been humiliated. At the same time, she was ashamed that she could preach about forgiveness but couldn't or wouldn't forgive. "Lord, forgive me. I can't forgive," she cried inwardly. As she prayed, she felt not only forgiven but set free. The glacier of hate melted within and her hand unfroze. As she reached out her hand and spoke her forgiveness, she felt another burden of the past fall away.

The cross is where we receive forgiveness and where we learn to forgive. Almost always, when we think about forgiveness, the Spirit flashes names and faces across the screens of our minds—a spouse, a friend, a parent, a child, an adversary. What do you need to bring to the cross, seeking the King's forgiveness? Who do you need to bring to the cross, seeking His power to forgive? The parable is not only powerful, it is pointed. It forces us to ask hard questions about our relationships and to live out our forgiveness, not only in thanksgiving but in forgiving.

# CHAPTER FIVE

# FINDING MY MASTER

As Alexander the Great was carrying his triumphant military campaign towards the East, he and a section of his army approached a strongly fortified, walled city. Alexander approached the city, demanded to see the king and set out terms of surrender. The king only laughed: "Why should I surrender to you? You can't do us any harm! We can endure any siege."

In response, Alexander offered to give the king a demonstration. Nearby, within sight of the city walls, was a sheer cliff. He ordered his men to line up in single file and began to march them towards the precipice. The city's citizens watched with horrified fascination as the column moved unhesitatingly towards and over the edge. Only after several men had plunged to their deaths did Alexander order the rest of the column to halt. He then called his troops back to his side and stood silently facing the city.

The effect on the citizens was stunning. From spellbound silence they moved to terror.

They realized they had no walls thick enough and no resources extensive enough to defend themselves against that kind of loyalty and commitment. Spontaneously they rushed through the gates to surrender themselves to Alexander.

It is impossible today to be sure of the authenticity of such a story. But there can be no doubt about the power of commitment. People loyal to a leader or a principle and willing to pay the price required will always overwhelm people who value comfort and convenience more than a cause. Our society generally does not breed strong commitment. The self-fulfillment ethic seduces us to believe that we have no higher loyalty than one to ourselves. The tragedy is that self-centered values eat away at commitment—not only at commitment to leaders and causes, but at commitments to marriage, family, and friends.

Believers are not immune to the world's value system. One missionary statesman has observed an irony of church life in the 1990s. While Third-World Christians are information-poor, they are commitment-rich. Sadly, Western Christians are information-rich, but they are commitment-poor. All generalizations are suspect, but that one seems to be uncomfortably true. Yet this condition collides with the plain teaching of Jesus. The demands of our master are incompatible with partial commitment or casual discipleship. The Lord's call to himself requires intelligent, unconditional allegiance to His person and work.

Jesus was always intensely realistic about what it meant to be His follower. He was never a huckster pushing a product while hiding the real costs in the fine print. Instead, He realistically spelled out His requirements, nowhere more clearly than in Luke 14:25–35. In this passage Jesus makes a different use of parables than we usually find. Normally the main point the Lord makes is made powerfully in the parable itself and needs little explanation. However, the parables of the careless builder and the careful king are used almost as a modern preacher would use a sermon illustration.

> Large crowds were traveling with Jesus, and turning to them he said: "If anyone comes to me and does not hate his father and mother, his wife and children, his brothers and sisters—yes, even his own life—he

cannot be my disciple. And anyone who does not carry his cross and follow me cannot be my disciple.

"Suppose one of you wants to build a tower. Will he not first sit down and estimate the cost to see if he has enough money to complete it? For if he lays the foundation and is not able to finish it, everyone who sees it will ridicule him, saying, 'This fellow began to build and was not able to finish.'

"Or suppose a king is about to go to war against another king. Will he not first sit down and consider whether he is able with ten thousand men to oppose the one coming against him with twenty thousand? If he is not able, he will send a delegation while the other is still a long way off and will ask for terms of peace. In the same way, any of you who does not give up everything he has cannot be my disciple.

"Salt is good, but if it loses its saltiness, how can it be made salty

again? It is fit neither for the soil nor
for the manure pile; it is thrown out.
"He who has ears to hear, let him
hear."

(Luke 14:25–35)

There is a phrase that rings through the
passage three times and makes the Lord's
message unmistakably clear: "he cannot be my
disciple . . . [he] cannot be my disciple . . . [he]
cannot be my disciple." Rather than actively
recruiting supporters for His program, the
Savior seems to be effectively discouraging
followers. Since He clearly desires people to
commit their lives to Him, His motivation must
be to enlist intelligent, realistic devotion.

The context in which Luke places this
story clarifies the Lord's motivation. What
immediately precedes is the parable of the
great banquet, a story that celebrates the free
grace of God. The gospel banquet is for all who
will accept the invitation. Immediately following
verses 25–35 are the three parables of seeking,
which describe God's joy in calling the unworthy
and the lost. There could be no clearer reminder
that salvation is by grace through faith. It is not

reserved for those who meet certain conditions, but is for any who will trust in Christ.

However, there are people whose relationship to Jesus is one of attachment without commitment. Luke tells us that "large crowds were traveling with Jesus." Physically, these people are on their way to Jerusalem in Jesus' entourage. But there is a suggestion that they are merely "going along" with Him spiritually as well. They certainly have beliefs about Him, but it is not clear that they truly believe in Him. Probably some are truly saved while others are not. Like many groups of people, this is a mixed company spiritually. But whatever their spiritual status, they need to understand the full implications of being a Christ-follower.

## The Conditions of Discipleship

Discipleship was common in the ancient world, roughly equivalent to our practice of apprenticeship. In a religious context, a disciple was a pupil who attached himself to a teacher or rabbi to acquire his religious knowledge and skill. He went through a process of training and testing, but his ultimate loyalty was not to his rabbi, but to the Torah and tradition. Because the Torah and tradition stood above the rabbi, a disciple would join himself to a teacher of his own choosing, much as a modern student makes the choice of a university. The disciple's real attachment was to the law and to a way of life.

Discipleship to Jesus is very different. The disciple's allegiance is not to the Torah and tradition but to the Lord himself. A disciple does not merely join the Jesus school, he binds himself in complete personal commitment to Him. Jesus' disciples do not merely choose; they are called, and they share not only in His message but also in His mission. A disciple is first someone who comes to Jesus in faith and trust (14:26). He comes for salvation to receive a free gift. But a disciple is also someone who follows Jesus. This is not a call to accept a certain way of life and to pass it on, as Jewish disciples did. It is not a call to adopt a philosophical position or a pattern of ritual behavior. It is rather a call to fellowship with Jesus and to obedient service for and to Him. As the Lord makes clear in verse 27, the way of discipleship is nothing less than the way of the cross.

It is sometimes debated whether the Lord's words here are addressed to believers or to unbelievers. That Jesus does address acknowledged believers in such terms and call them to deeper commitment is clear from Luke 9:18–27. Discipleship is not the same thing as salvation. While every believer should be a disciple, not every one is in the sense given here. But it is also unlikely that everyone whom the Lord addresses is already saved. In the mixed company of verse 25 are some who need to be shocked into realizing that casual attachment is not enough. They profess some type of commitment to the Lord, but the Savior's unqualified demands force them to examine the reality of that commitment.

Jesus speaks first in unequivocal terms about the loyalty He requires of disciples, a loyalty that transcends all human relationships. "If anyone comes to me and does not hate his father and mother, his wife and children, his brothers and sisters—yes, even his own life—he cannot be my disciple." The language is shocking. After all, this is the same man who has spoken of the great commandment, "Love your neighbor as yourself" (Matt. 22:34–40) and who has excoriated the Pharisees for their failure truly to honor father and mother (Matt. 15:1–9). Two things help us understand the Lord's meaning.

"Hate" in this context does not mean actual ill will, but is a comparative, as revealed by the use of the term in Genesis 29:30–31. In verse 30, we are told that Jacob "loved Rachel more than Leah." The next verse is translated, "When the LORD saw that Leah was not loved," but the Hebrew term is "hated." Jacob did not actually "hate" Leah, but he did love her less than he did Rachel, an emotional choice that, no doubt, felt like hatred to Leah. In a very similar passage in Matthew 10:37, the Lord says, "Anyone who loves his father or mother more than me is not worthy of me."

Jesus is indicating that He demands a priority in our relationships. I must love nothing or no one more than I love Him. Families represent the very best things in life. They are God-given, and I am to love them more than anything else, with the sole exception of my love for Christ. This does not mean that I will demean my family or neglect it. The very opposite is true if I take Scripture seriously. But no relationship, no matter how wonderful, must compete with my allegiance to the Lord.

As a high school student Francis Schaeffer came to Christ. He came from a non-religious family, and when his father became aware that

his son wanted to go to college to train for
the ministry, he expressed violent opposition.
Schaeffer felt torn between love for his Lord
and love for his father, but prayer only made
his sense of direction clearer. One day his
father met him at the door with the words,
"I don't want a son who is a minister, and I
don't want you to go." Schaeffer went off to
pray but returned to his father with the simple
statement, "Dad, I've got to go." Enraged, his
father slammed the door in his face. Schaeffer
later commented that few choices had been
more costly than the decision about whether
to please the Lord or his father. His father
returned minutes later to declare that, although
he disagreed, he would still pay for his son's
first year. But Schaeffer's choice of loyalties,
difficult as it was, bore rich dividends. It laid
the foundation for a fruitful ministry, and it also
resulted in his father's eventual salvation.

Discipleship not only deals with personal
relationships, it also addresses personal goals.
"Anyone who does not carry his cross and
follow me cannot be my disciple." The picture
is one a first-century Jew, in a land occupied
by the Romans, could not misunderstand.
A person carrying a cross is on his way to

execution. Sentence has already been passed, his future has already been decided, and the end is only moments away. The cross is not a symbol of the comparatively trivial burdens and problems of life. It speaks of humiliation, excruciating pain, and certain death. The image would have sent a shudder of fear through the Lord's hearers.

Is Christ speaking of actual physical death? That is a real possibility for some, but there is a nuance in the text that points in a different direction for most. The present tenses describe a continuing process; in effect, "anyone who does not keep on carrying his cross and keep on following me." The Lord Jesus is the supreme cross-bearer, denying himself continually and living in submission to His Father's will. In this sense, He had been a cross-bearer long before He walked the way to Golgotha. His goals had been determined by His Father, not himself, and that way has always meant suffering and rejection. The cross-bearing disciple has chosen to follow in the steps of his Lord. Therefore, his life is shaped by the mission of his Lord, not by his own goals and desires.

To take the cross then is a continuing and voluntary act in which God's will and Christ's mission determine one's life. As James Denney once wrote, "The man who has nothing to die for has nothing to live for; he does not know what life is." The disciple, however, has everything to live for, because he has chosen what and who he will die for. His life has been placed at the full disposal of the Lord Jesus.

These are strong words, hard to accept in a society that insists on self-realization as life's goal and personal preference as life's guide. Today the cross is a decoration or an ornament. But Jesus is not asking us to wear a necklace. He is calling us to a radical and costly identification with Him. However, the cross will not be forced upon us. We choose to take it up out of devotion to the Lord himself.

## The Cost of Discipleship

At this point, Jesus gives us two brief parables. Both of them involve paying a price, taking a risk. A disciple is gambling everything in life on the Lord Jesus. Wise people do not make such choices impulsively or recklessly. Besides, impulsive commitment will almost certainly lack endurance.

The first parable tells the story of a careless builder. Almost every city has a half-finished monument to carelessness; during its economic recession, the city of Dallas was dotted with structures begun in days of prosperity, whose unfinished condition bore witness to inadequate resources. The Lord's picture is not of a metropolitan skyscraper but of a farmer's tower, probably in a vineyard. The wise builder, the Lord suggests, will "estimate the cost to see if he has enough money to complete it." He will make a careful evaluation of the costs, risks, and resources. Otherwise, the unfinished structure will be visible evidence of impulsive commitment, and his failure will expose him to ridicule.

The application is obvious. Discipleship is not a casual or an occasional activity. Enthusiasm for it is important, but that will be insufficient to sustain a man plodding under the burden of the cross. Discipleship is an exciting adventure, but it is also a draining and demanding lifestyle. Warfare looks thrilling in the movies; it looks very different from the trenches. "Count the cost—it is no small matter to build a life for Me."

The second parable poses a very different problem. If it is foolish to begin without counting the cost, it is disastrous to delay one's choice without considering the consequences. The Lord portrays a king who is being invaded by an army twice the size of his. The enemy is already on the march, and he must decide whether to resist or not. His position and resources may be enough. Armies of ten thousand have often defeated larger, more powerful armies. But what if he fights and loses? One thing he does not have is limitless time to ponder. He must weigh the risks, make his choice, and live with the consequences. If he delays in making a decision, he will have a fight whether he wants one or not. If battle means defeat, then delay in seeking peace will be catastrophic.

Again the Lord's point is obvious. Not only do we need to count the cost of discipleship, we need to consider the consequences of refusing discipleship. One way or another, choice is inevitable. Not to decide is to decide not to become a disciple. And not to become a disciple is to miss the privilege of knowing and following the Lord Jesus. It is to default on participating in His mission and sharing His victories. Paradoxically, it is to say no to life itself. "For whoever wants to save his life will lose it, but whoever loses his life for me will save it" (Luke 9:24). The life of a disciple may be extremely demanding, but it is also infinitely satisfying.

The two pictures are complementary: count the costs of discipleship; consider the consequences of refusing discipleship. There is a price to be paid either way. Completing that idea, the Lord concludes, "In the same way, any of you who does not give up everything he has cannot be my disciple." Discipleship not only demands my personal relationships (9:26) and my personal preferences (9:27), it also demands my personal resources. I am to "give up everything" I have. Please note: I am to "give it up," not "give it away." The Lord is not asking me to give "away" my home or my wife. But I am to "give them up," or, as the same verb is translated in Luke 9:61, to "say good-bye" to them. This is a call to sign over my family and the title for my property to the Lord, to yield ownership. Disciples give authority over their relationships, their possessions, and their resources to Christ. All that I have is to be used consistently with His mission and direction. My house becomes His house; my car, His car; my savings, His savings.

This renunciation is a costly act for those of us who love the "stuff" of life. It is also a continual act, as the tense of the Greek verb suggests: "keeps on giving up everything he has!" Quite personally, this was a price of discipleship I found much easier to deal with when I was a college student than now when I have college students of my own. The things we own often come to own us. Discipleship involves a daily act of signing away ownership.

## The Commitment of Discipleship

The Lord completes His challenge with a reminder of who disciples are and how they are to function in the world. "Salt is good." Salt was a commodity of great value in the biblical world. It was recognized as essential to life and was used in the preservation of food, as a purifying agent and antiseptic against corruption and decay, as a seasoning, and even as a fertilizer for certain types of plants and soil. In earlier times, soldiers received their wages (*salary*) in salt; covenants were made based on salt; and major trade routes were established for the exchange of salt.

But salt could become saltless. The Lord does not mean that sodium chloride could cease to be sodium chloride. The salt used in Palestine, however, was not the refined product found in our modern stores. Lumps of material that once contained true salt could look like salt, but the sodium chloride had been leached away. Such material was virtually useless. It might be spread on roads as a primitive paving material, but that was about all. There was little productive use to which such "saltless salt" could be put.

Believers function as the salt of the earth (Matt. 5:13). They are the Lord's intended moral preservatives and seasoning agents for the world. But the essence of our saltiness is our discipleship, our unconditional commitment to Christ as Lord of our personal relationships, personal preferences, and personal goals. Without discipleship, the Christian is saltless salt, useless to achieve divine objectives. Our usefulness depends on our spiritual distinctiveness, and our distinctiveness is our unqualified commitment to our Lord.

The privilege of being a disciple of Jesus Christ is the greatest available to a human being. That privilege is available freely, but not everyone will qualify. About some, the Lord bluntly says, "He cannot be my disciple."

That refusal is not on the basis of deficient intelligence, insufficient talent, or limited resources. Disciples are not required to be smart, gifted, or rich, but they do need to be loyal and unconditionally committed to Jesus.

Count the cost. Are you building carelessly or carefully? Consider the consequences—are you choosing actively or drifting dangerously?

At the turn of the century, a speaker at a great student missionary convention spoke words that resonate down through the years:

> Most people are not satisfied with the permanent output of their lives. Nothing can wholly satisfy the life of Christ within His followers except the adoption of Christ's purposes toward the world. Fame, pleasure and riches are but husks and actions in contrast with the boundless and abiding joy of working with God for the fulfillment of His eternal plans. The people who are putting everything into Christ's undertakings are getting out of life its simplest and most priceless rewards.

Such is the life of a disciple. Count the cost—are you careless or careful? Consider the consequences—to delay is to default.

In 1945, Alexander Solzhenitsyn was arrested on political charges and began eleven years of misery in Stalin's prisons. Describing the tortures he and other prisoners endured, he gave his prescription for survival:

> So what is the answer? How can you stand your ground when you are weak and sensitive to pain, when people you love are still alive, when you are unprepared? What do you need to make you stronger than the interrogator and the whole trap? From the moment you go to prison you must put your cozy past firmly behind you. At the very threshold, you must say to yourself: "My life is over, a little early to be sure, but there's nothing to be done about it. I shall never return to freedom. I am condemned to die—now or a little later. But later on, in truth, it will be even harder, and so the sooner the better. I no longer have any property whatsoever. For

me those I love have died, and for
them I have died. From today on, my
body is useless and alien to me. Only
my spirit and my conscience remain
precious and important to me." Confronted by such a prisoner, the inter-
rogation will tremble. Only the man
who has renounced everything can
win that victory.

(The Gulag Archipelago)

Undoubtedly there is power in renunciation.
But that is not the Lord's secret. The power of
discipleship is not the strength of what we say
no to, but the power of whom we say yes to.

Count the cost! Consider the consequences!
Embrace the opportunity!

# CHAPTER SIX

# ACCUMULATING MY TREASURE

Like every other child, I knew what it was to go running into the house, tears streaming down my face because someone had insulted me and called me a name. As my mother wiped away my tears, she would also try to wipe away the pain with the refrain, "Sticks and stones may break my bones, but names will never hurt me." But when the tables turned and she heard me calling my brothers or my playmates names, her attitude was very different! Then she told me how hurtful names were. As discipline was applied to the most vulnerable part of my anatomy, I was told in the plainest terms that such language was wrong, and I was never to speak that way again. Instinctively, I knew that my mother was closer to the truth in the latter case than in the former. Names hurt, and they keep on hurting, especially if they hit the mark.

I still hate being called names. Words can wound and even kill. But sometimes they break through pretense and expose things as they really are. Truth in labeling is sometimes an act of love, a harsh kindness we must hear. High on the list of hurtful names is the word "fool," especially when it is used by God. To be a fool in God's eyes is to have missed the point of life. The remarkable thing is that the person God calls a fool, we would very often call a success, a person to be envied.

The 1980s will probably go down in American history as "the decade of the yuppies." Much as an earlier era chanted "You can have it all," the yuppie slogan became "You should have it all." The early part of the decade was marked by acquisition and consumption. Economic downturns later shifted the emphasis from the pursuit of "more" to the pursuit of security. But materialism reigned supreme—and it was not confined to yuppies. A study of contemporary American youth by the Cooperative Research Program in 1988 concluded that "they are overwhelmingly materialistic; interested more than ever primarily in making money" (*Trinity Journal*, Fall 1988, p. 216) A breed of preachers baptized this impulse into a "health, wealth, and prosperity" theology, epitomized by one preacher's question, "If the Mafia can ride around in Lincoln Continental town cars, why can't the King's kids?"

Baby boomers did not invent the pursuit of possessions, although they certainly have refined the art. And our time will probably not be characterized by any radical turning from materialism. We have been nurtured in a society that seduces with the promise of affluence and measures worth on the basis of possessions and positions. There is nothing inherently wrong with professional success, financial security, or personal prosperity. But at some point, a follower of Jesus Christ crosses the line into enemy territory. As the Lord has told us, we cannot be His disciples unless we say good-bye to all our possessions (Luke 14:33).

The Lord once told a group of Pharisees, described as people "who loved money," that "what is highly valued among men is detestable in God's sight" (Luke 16:15). Undoubtedly, we value the fruits of being well-to-do and successful. Could it be that Jesus detests what I aspire to? He has a very painful way of probing the central nervous system of my life. In the parable of the rich fool, found in Luke 12:13–21,

He forces all of us to face some searching
questions about ourselves.

> Someone in the crowd said to him,
> "Teacher, tell my brother to divide the
> inheritance with me."
> Jesus replied, "Man, who appoint-
> ed me a judge or an arbiter between
> you?" Then he said to them, "Watch
> out! Be on your guard against all
> kinds of greed; a man's life does
> not consist in the abundance of his
> possessions."
> And he told them this parable:
> "The ground of a certain rich man
> produced a good crop. He thought
> to himself, 'What shall I do? I have no
> place to store my crops.'
> Then he said, 'This is what I'll do.
> I will tear down my barns and build
> bigger ones, and there I will store all
> my grain and my goods. And I'll say
> to myself, "You have plenty of good
> things laid up for many years. Take
> life easy; eat, drink and be merry." '
> "But God said to him, 'You fool!
> This very night your life will be

demanded from you. Then who
will get what you have prepared for
yourself?'

"This is how it will be with anyone
who stores up things for himself but
is not rich toward God."

## Probing the Heart: The Warning of the Lord

As Jesus moved toward Jerusalem, huge
crowds were drawn to Him. Luke tells us that
"a crowd of many thousands had gathered, so
that they were trampling on one another" (Luke
12:1). At the same time, His enemies had begun
"to oppose him fiercely and to besiege him with
questions, waiting to catch him in something
he might say" (Luke 11:53–54). In that context
of popular acclaim and deep hostility, the Lord
called His disciples to bold and fearless witness
on His behalf (Luke 12:1–3).

One of the men in the crowd had little interest
in such matters. He had come with a family
problem, related to an inheritance. Apparently
he was the younger of two brothers. According
to Jewish law, his older brother would have
been both the executor of the estate and the
largest recipient of the inheritance and would
usually have tried to maintain the estate intact.

But that wasn't the younger brother's plan. He wanted money of his own to use as he pleased. Since it was common to bring disputed points of the law to an accredited rabbi, he blurted out his concern to Jesus: "Teacher, tell my brother to divide the inheritance with me." His words are revealing. He doesn't ask the Lord to make a judgment, but to side with him to provide ammunition against his brother. Like many since his time, he wants to use Jesus to meet his monetary desires.

The Lord refuses to be drawn into such a role: "Man, who appointed me a judge or an arbiter between you?" Jesus has no legal standing as an accredited rabbi to be involved in such cases. But more importantly, such a task is no part of His divine mission. As Leon Morris observes, "He came to bring men to God, not property to man" (*The Gospel According to St. Luke*, p. 212). That is an important truth to embrace when some teach us that believers can and should expect the Lord to provide physical well-being and prosperity. Even if this man is being wronged by his brother, getting his rights may not be best for him. There is a deeper issue involved, and a greater danger than being cheated out of one's inheritance.

It is that danger the Lord has in mind as He turns from the man to the multitudes ("to *them*"): "Watch out! Be on your guard against all kinds of greed; a man's life does not consist in the abundance of his possessions." The initial words, "Watch out! Be on your guard!" put the Lord's message in neon lights. This is not an abstract possibility or a theoretical concern. What Jesus has in view is not just a sin, but a serious, yet subtle, sin. Some sins are clear and recognizable, and evangelicals are quick to label them as evil and condemn participation in them. Rarely do we see greed as a horrific sin. But remarkably, Jesus never warns about adultery and drunkenness in such dramatic terms as He uses here against covetousness.

In the days following her flight from the Philippines with her deposed husband, revelations about Imelda Marcos made her name a synonym for greed. What can a woman do with thousands of pairs of shoes? But the Imelda Marcos syndrome operates throughout the economic scale. The term "greed" means simply "a consuming desire to have more"; it has the nuance of a grasping for more, a lust to acquire. It is the very opposite of the contentment that accompanies true godliness (1 Tim. 6:6). Someone once asked John D. Rockefeller how much money was enough. "One dollar more," he replied. The beast of greed is never full. It is insatiable.

We miss the point, however, if we see covetousness as an issue of amount not attitude. The poorest can be greedy; the richest can avoid greed. But the danger of possessions is that they often arouse the desire for more. Ivan Boesky, who went to prison and paid a fine of $100 million for insider trading was, a few years earlier, the darling of Wall Street. During that time he declared at a graduation ceremony at a major university, "Greed is all right. I want you to know I think greed is healthy. You can be greedy and still feel good about yourself." As *Newsweek* later commented, "The strangest thing when we look back will not be just that Ivan Boesky could say that at a business school graduation, but that it was greeted with laughter and applause" (Dec. 1, 1986).

But greed is no laughing matter. It is, in fact, idolatry (Col. 3:5). The Lord leaves no doubt. "A man's life does not consist in the abundance of his possessions" (Luke 12:15). God alone is the source of life; God alone controls life; God alone gives life. In the 1950s, wrestling was almost as popular as it is at present (and just as authentic!). The European champion was Yussif the Turk, who came to America to fight Strangler Lewis for the "world championship" and $5,000. Yussif won and insisted that the $5,000 be paid in gold, which he stuffed into his championship belt. The money mattered so much that he refused to remove the belt until he had reached home safely. Boarding the first available ship to Europe, he headed home. But halfway across the Atlantic, the ship foundered in a storm and began to sink. In a panic, Yussif jumped for a lifeboat, missed, and went straight to the bottom. His golden belt had become a golden anchor, a vivid illustration of the Lord's words.

## Portraying the Problem: The Rich Fool

The Lord is not content to give us an abstract warning. In the parable of the rich fool, he introduces us to a first-century yuppie. Wealth often begets wealth, and his wealth enabled him to possess land that produced a bumper crop. There seems to be no criticism intended by the fact of his wealth, his manner of acquiring it, or its increase. What is decisive is what he chooses to do with it. Even then, it is not his actions so much as his assumptions that are crucial. Given his values, building bigger barns is a wise, pragmatic decision. Yet that is precisely the question: what are his values?

Three things define this man. The first is *selfishness*: "I . . . I . . . I"—six times over. He is totally preoccupied with himself. For him, the purpose of having is self-indulgence. "I deserve it; I owe it to myself; I'll do it my way"—all the anthems and slogans of twenty-first century selfists were known to their first-century cousins. The second is *materialism*. The purpose of having barns is to get bigger barns, and the good life comes from having good things. The quality of the future he anticipates is directly related to the size of the barns he builds. He could no more be content with medium-sized barns than Imelda Marcos could be content with ten pairs of shoes. Third, his life is characterized by *hedonism*. "I'll say to myself, '. . . take life easy; eat, drink and be merry.' " We should not miss the Lord's point. Solomon tells us that it is a gift of God "that everyone may eat and drink, and find satisfaction in all his toil" (Eccl. 3:13). Paul tells us that our gracious God "provides us with everything for our enjoyment" (1 Tim. 6:17). It is right to enjoy what we have; it is wrong to believe that self-indulgent pleasure is the goal of life, as this man does. He believes that his wealth makes him master both of the present and the future.

We can summarize his view of life in several phrases that ring through the years: "If I'm not good to myself, who will be?" "Success with possessions shows I'm a success as a person." "The bigger the barn (or car or house), the better the life." "If money can't buy happiness, it can at least buy pleasure and security."

But, in a moment, the bubble bursts. God passes sentence not only on the rich fool but on every life based upon covetousness. " 'You fool! This very night your life will be demanded from you. Then who will get what you have prepared for yourself?' " The Lord's diagnosis is unrelenting in its honesty and revealing in its insights. Three things stand out.

## 1. He is a fool, not a success.

Almost certainly, in the community's eyes, he is a man to be envied. In God's eyes, he is a fool to be pitied. The term *fool* in biblical language is not a description of mental ability but of spiritual discernment. In the Old

Testament language of Psalms and Proverbs,
a fool is an individual who makes choices as
if God doesn't exist and who lives as if God
hasn't spoken. Eleven times over, we hear "I"
and "my" in this man's words. For all intents and
purposes, God does not exist.

## 2. He is a servant, not a master.

The rich man is convinced that he is in
control of his life and that wealth gives him
control. But God's words to him make it clear
that he has no power over the present: "This
very night your life will be demanded from you."
The word *demanded* is a commercial term,
used of a loan. At this crisis point he discovers
a truth that everyone learns sooner or later.
God owns life, and He merely loans our earthly
existence to us. At any time He can call in His
loan. The fool also has no power over the future:
"Who will get what you have prepared for
yourself?" As the writer of Ecclesiastes laments,
"I must leave [my wealth] to the one who comes
after me. And who knows whether he will be a
wise man or a fool?" (Eccl. 2:18–19).

## 3. He is a pauper, not a rich man.

In the moment of truth, the wealthy farmer
realizes that he has worked so hard for so

little. He has invested in the passing, not in the permanent. What makes death hard is the evaluation of what we lose by it. This is a man who is leaving everything behind—the barns he has built, the people he has controlled, the prestige he has acquired. Death strips him bare and reveals him for who he is, a man who "stores up things for himself but is not rich toward God."

That last statement forces us to sober reflection. Am I a fool in God's eyes? What label would He attach to my life? Jim Elliot's familiar words merit careful consideration: "He is no fool who gives what he cannot keep to gain what he cannot lose."

There is another type of foolishness the Lord wants us to recognize. He has described in the parable the folly that says "God doesn't matter" and "I can't get enough." The power of possessions is that they give us a feeling of control. But disciples face another folly, the folly that says "God doesn't care." We are tempted to believe that if we follow the Lord, renouncing all our possessions, we may not have enough.

## Presenting the Alternative: Treasure That Endures

Then Jesus said to his disciples: "Therefore I tell you, do not worry about your life, what you will eat; or about your body, what you will wear. Life is more than food, and the body more than clothes. Consider the ravens: They do not sow or reap, they have no storeroom or barn; yet God feeds them. And how much more valuable you are than birds! Who of you by worrying can add a single hour to his life? Since you cannot do this very little thing, why do you worry about the rest?

"Consider how the lilies grow. They do not labor or spin. Yet I tell you, not even Solomon in all his splendor was dressed like one of these. If that is how God clothes the grass of the field, which is here today, and tomorrow is thrown into the fire, how much more will he clothe you, O you of little faith! And do not set your heart on what you will eat or drink; do not

worry about it. For the pagan world
runs after all such things, and your
Father knows that you need them.
But seek his kingdom, and these
things will be given to you as well.

"Do not be afraid, little flock, for
your Father has been pleased to give
you the kingdom. Sell your possessions and give to the poor. Provide
purses for yourselves that will not
wear out, a treasure in heaven that
will not be exhausted, where no thief
comes near and no moth destroys.
For where your treasure is, there your
heart will be also." (Luke 12:22–34)

Luke makes it very clear that this section is
addressed not to the crowd but to the disciples.
There is an implication here that worry is one
of the besetting sins of Christ-followers. The
reason is not hard to discover. The terms of
discipleship are demanding. To obey the call
is to trust Christ completely, but what are
the implications of that obedience? Financial
questions also loom large. If I say good-bye to
all my possessions, will the Lord really meet my
needs? My head assures me that He will; my

heart is not quite so certain. "An anxious heart weighs a man down" (Prov. 12:25). Physically, this is so. As someone has observed, people get ulcers not so much from what they eat as from what eats them. Anxiety also steals emotional peace and removes spiritual assurance.

Worry is not the presence of appropriate concern for life's responsibilities. Rather, it is undue care, exaggerated concern. Although the Lord illustrates His words by making a comparison to birds who work but neither worry nor plan, He is not asking us to live on the level of the birds. The people to whom the Lord is speaking know what it is to scramble for life's necessities. Life was hard in biblical Palestine, roughly equivalent to peasant life in a Third World country today. The needs of life did not fall into their hands accidently, nor were they delivered by a benevolent government. The old King James translation, "Take no thought for your life," seriously misrepresents the verb the Lord uses. He is not calling for thoughtlessness or the absence of appropriate concern. The sense of the word is beautifully illustrated in the complaint of Martha to Jesus about her sister Mary's lack of assistance. Martha, we read, "was distracted by all the preparations that had to be made" (Luke 10:40). She was totally unable to enjoy the Lord's presence because her mind was divided by other responsibilities. (The Greek word for *worry* literally means "to divide the mind." The Latin root of our word *anxiety* is *angere*, "to choke, be in distress.") So Jesus' words to her are "Martha, Martha, you are worried and upset about many things." Anxiety is the emotional distraction and distress that comes from allowing the duties and the unknowns of life to absorb and control us.

Telling us not to worry isn't very helpful. People who tell us that usually seem either unrealistic, uninformed, or patronizing. The Lord forces us to think about why we are not to worry. First, He tells us that worry is foolish (12:22–24). It is falling into the folly of the rich fool who believed that his life consisted of his possessions. But life is more than food and clothes, and God has promised us that He will care for us, much more so than He does for His creatures, the birds. To worry is foolishly to forget who we are—God's valued children, and who He is—our loving Father. Second, worry is futile (12:25–28). Worry can shorten life, but it can't lengthen it—and God who gives beauty to the fields will not strip us bare. Anxiety denies the care of God, and all to no effect. So the alternative is not to be "care-less" but "trust-full." A little bit of reflection helps us to recognize that most worry is about things that can't be changed (the past), things that can't be controlled (the present), or things that might not happen (the future). How much better to entrust ourselves to our God! Third, worry is faithless (12:29–31). To be absorbed with physical and personal needs is ultimately to be captured by unbelief. If the gospel is really true, our lives should be different qualitatively from the lives of pagans.

In his book *Run Today's Race*, Oswald Chambers observes that "all of our fret and worry is caused by calculating without God." Worry is the product of an inadequate understanding of our Father. He is the One who knows, cares, and acts. The way we look at God determines the way we will look at life, and this will determine what we worry about. Our great need is to worry about the right thing. What is that? "Seek his kingdom." We do not refrain from worrying. We replace concern about secondary things with concern about the primary thing. Only His kingdom is worthy of our ultimate concern.

The conjoined twin of anxiety is fear, and the Lord addresses fear in verses 32–34. He calls us to take drastic action with our financial resources and personal possessions. We are not to grasp them or trust them. We are rather to dispose of them by investing them eternally. In fact, the only way we can truly protect our treasures is to invest them in heaven. Our hearts follow our treasure, and if our treasure is in heaven, so will our hearts be. As David Gooding writes, "Heaven is scarcely a reality to a man who is not prepared to invest hard cash in it and in its interests; but by that same token it becomes more of a reality to the man who is" (*According to Luke*, p. 241).

The crucial issue in life is not the *amount* of our treasure, but the *location* of it. The rich man's treasures were on earth. He was a fool because he built his life around what couldn't last and what really didn't matter. The disciple's call is to be rich toward God, with a treasure in heaven that will not be exhausted. D. L. Moody once said, "It does not take long to tell where a man's treasure is. In fifteen minutes' conversation with most men, you can tell whether their treasures are on earth or in heaven."

No one wants to be called a fool by God. How do we make sure that doesn't happen? We can choose limits, not luxury, so our treasure can be invested in heaven. We can cultivate compassion, not greed. Most of all, we can pursue confidence in God, not money. On our money we Americans print the slogan "In God we trust." Fine words—but do we trust God *on* our money or *with* our money? Writing of his slim financial resources in a time of escalating needs, a friend said, "If we find ourselves sinking, we will not cry 'uncle.' Instead, we will cry out 'Father' to the One who knows all our needs and possesses all resources." Such a person has learned the wisdom of God.

## CHAPTER SEVEN

# ASSURING MY FUTURE

I am sure that I do not want to be called a fool by the Lord Jesus. But I have mixed feelings about another word He uses—one He wants to apply to my life. It is the term *shrewd*. The English word sometimes means someone who is astute and discerning. In such usage it describes a virtue. But very often it describes someone who is tricky and cunning. That it is used to describe a disciple surprises me. When I hear the word, I make all kinds of mental associations. I tend to think of a shrewd lawyer as someone who knows all the loopholes and is carefully legal but unconcerned about moral principle or true justice. *Shrewd* is the way we describe a cunning businessman who knows how to exploit his competitor's weakness or a customer's ignorance. In the early development of the English language *shrewd* meant "wicked," while today it denotes someone who is "wily and astute." The shrewd person is the clear-eyed, hard-nosed individual who knows how to play the angles and work the system for a competitive edge and for future benefits. *Shrewd* takes us into the cut-and-thrust of political negotiations and high-stakes business deals.

Our perceptions of the Lord Jesus tend to be of someone who is passive and other-worldly. Pictures of Him inevitably show Him wearing a white garment, brighter and cleaner than anyone else's. We have a hard time seeing Him with sweat on his forehead, callouses on His hands, and dirt under His fingernails. We have an even harder time seeing Him as a tradesman, negotiating with suppliers and customers over prices, balancing the books, and paying His taxes at the end of the year. But those things were every bit as much a part of His earthly life as the Sermon on the Mount or the feeding of the five thousand.

Still, the idea that followers of Christ are to be "shrewd" is a little unsettling. Our concept of discipleship is more comfortable with descriptions like "meek," "gentle," "nice," "mild." In certain contexts those are entirely appropriate descriptions. But we miss another side of God's will if we do not balance these with characteristics like "realistic," "astute," "tough," and, yes, "shrewd." These terms concern the very "this-worldly" issue of how we handle money and our material possessions.

One of the most common features of our Lord's parables is their shock value. They surprise and startle. The "heroes" are the most unexpected people. That is particularly true of the parable of the unrighteous steward, found in Luke 16:1–13. It is a story that has stirred controversy and debate among interpreters. But despite the questions it has raised, it confronts us with an essential truth about life as a disciple. The parable is given first in verses 1–8a and is followed by the Lord's elaboration of the principles the story is intended to teach.

## The Parable of the Shrewd, Dishonest Manager (Luke 16:1–8a)

> Jesus told his disciples: "There was a rich man whose manager was accused of wasting his possessions. So he called him in and asked him, 'What is this I hear about you? Give an account of your management, because you cannot be manager any longer.'
>
> "The manager said to himself, 'What shall I do now? My master is

taking away my job. I'm not strong enough to dig, and I'm ashamed to beg—I know what I'll do so that, when I lose my job here, people will welcome me into their houses.'

"So he called in each one of his master's debtors. He asked the first, 'How much do you owe my master?' 'Eight hundred gallons of olive oil,' he replied.

"The manager told him, 'Take your bill, sit down quickly, and make it four hundred.'

"Then he asked the second, 'And how much do you owe?' 'A thousand bushels of wheat,' he replied.

"He told him, 'Take your bill and make it eight hundred.' The master commended the dishonest manager because he had acted shrewdly."

In chapter 15, Luke has given us the three great parables of the Father who seeks the lost. The parable that opens chapter 16 is not related by Luke historically to what precedes it. There is, however, a thematic connection in that the prodigal son "squandered his wealth," while this manager is found guilty of squandering his master's possessions (16:1). But the two parables that compose most of chapter 16— this one and the following story of the rich man and Lazarus—deal with financial matters. It is significant that, while the story is addressed to the Lord's disciples, Luke is careful to observe that "the Pharisees, who loved money, heard all this and were sneering at Jesus." Clearly, what He requires is not a way of life that will appeal to a person who loves money. The gauntlet is thrown down: Serve God or Money. They are two rival gods, and you cannot serve both.

The parable takes us into the world of finance and responsibility. The manager is a steward. That is, he is an employee, perhaps of an absentee landlord, who has been given control over his master's business and assets. Clearly, his responsibility is to use this trust to further his master's interests, not his own. But the temptation to divert funds for his own purposes and pleasures proves too strong. He wastes the money, violating his trust and mishandling his master's possessions. News of his malfeasance reaches his employer, and, when confronted with the charge of dereliction of duty, the man has no answer to give.

To this point, there is a great similarity to another of the Lord's stories, the parable of the unforgiving servant, recorded in Matthew 18. The repetition of these circumstances shows that violation of trust was just as common in the ancient world as it is today. Certainly the man deserves to be fired from his job. But it is important to notice the manager's precise position after his master's words: "Give an account of your management, because you cannot be manager any longer." Modern companies generally tell fired employees to clean out their desks immediately, or they have it done for them. But this man is given a window of opportunity. His dismissal is inevitable, but it is not yet final or public. Until the account is rendered, he has some room for movement. Still, time is short, and immediate action is imperative. He has no time to waste.

It is here that the man's shrewdness is revealed. He knows his options are limited. He is too weak for manual labor, and he is too proud to beg. Unless he acts quickly, one of those might be his fate. But he knows the adage, "Scratch my back, and I'll scratch yours." Perhaps he can do favors for a few people, so that they will be beholden to him.

His plan is very simple. He begins to call in his master's customers and alter their bills. After all, he has managed the accounts and still has legal authority to act on his master's behalf. "How much do you owe?" "Eight hundred gallons of olive oil." "Here's your old I.O.U. Rewrite it, put down four hundred gallons and I'll sign it." "How much do you owe?" "A thousand bushels of wheat." "Here, make it eight hundred. I'll sign it."

We don't know enough about first-century business practices to be certain of what is going on here. Some commentators are convinced that the whole business is fraudulent and that he is implicating these people in cheating his boss. That is possible, but since these people would presumably continue to do business with the rich man, it seems rather unlikely. It is more likely that the transaction is subtle and semi-legal. According to Mosaic law, Jewish businessmen were not allowed to charge interest to fellow Jews. But that made commercial transactions difficult. So a subterfuge often was followed. When money was loaned, it was illegal to write a bill stating any interest. So written bills generally showed only one amount, the principal loaned plus the interest and the manager's fees. This amount was often stated in terms of commodities (oil, wheat), rather than money. In this way, it would appear that the law was being followed.

If this is so, what the steward is probably doing is discounting the face value of the notes by suspending the interest charges. Since these charges are not legal within Jewish law, his master has no ground of action against him. Presumably, the debtors would be suspicious of the reasons but would accept the offer gladly. He has therefore tied his master's hands effectively, stayed within the bounds of legality, and ingratiated himself with people he wants to remember him kindly.

The parable closes with the statement, "The master commended the dishonest manager because he had acted shrewdly." It is important to see what is and is not said. The master does not say that he is pleased by his steward's actions, but that he is impressed. The manager has tied the man's hands and achieved his own ends. The master certainly does not commend the manager's earlier dishonesty, but, like a defeated athlete commenting wryly on his opponent's skill and strategy, he feels compelled to acknowledge the man's success.

Since the word *shrewd* is the key to the story, it is important to consider its meaning carefully. The Greek word means "to act with foresight," and is illustrated in Jesus' discourse by the wise man (literally, the shrewd man) who built his house on the rock in anticipation of a coming storm (Matt. 7:24). It also describes the five "wise" (shrewd) virgins (Matt. 25:1–13), who bring extra oil anticipating future need. This is the dishonest manager's quality; he acts decisively in the present to position himself for the future. His behavior is consistent with his circumstances. He recognizes his crisis and seizes his opportunity because he has his eye on the future, not just the present. He is astute enough to act with practical cleverness and judgment.

The story is troubling. This man seems to be an unlikely hero. In fact, he is not a hero at all. But in his actions, dubious as they are, we can see a quality demonstrated which disciples require if they are to live effectively in the world. That quality is elaborated in the Lord's continuing discussion.

## The Principles of Shrewd Discipleship (Luke 16:8b–13)

"For the people of this world are more shrewd in dealing with their own kind than are the people of the light. I tell you, use worldly wealth to gain friends for yourselves, so that when it is gone, you will be welcomed into eternal dwellings.

"Whoever can be trusted with very little can also be trusted with much, and whoever is dishonest with very little will also be dishonest with much. So if you have not been trustworthy in handling worldly wealth, who will trust you with true riches? And if you have not been trustworthy with some-one else's property, who will give you property of your own?

"No servant can serve two mas-ters. Either he will hate the one and love the other, or he will be devoted to the one and despise the other. You cannot serve both God and Money."

A recent trip took me to the jungles of northern Liberia. The simple villages were a long way from civilization as I knew it. I understood why missionaries were there, taking the eternal gospel to needy people. But the products of American business were there as well, sold by store owners who seemed to be everywhere, pursuing commerce. The Lord's words remind us that this is characteristic of the people of this world. They are shrewd in dealing with temporal things. They see the possibilities and seize the opportunities. They sacrifice present comforts for future prospects.

Sadly, "the people of the light" are often less than shrewd. Unbelievers outpace disciples in their foresight, their ingenuity, and their risk-taking. They study their world, see the opportunities, and seize them, knowing that opportunities missed are usually opportunities lost. Too often, God's people are lethargic or uncreative or unstrategic in their thinking. We spend money, but do not use it well. Our planning is careless; our strategy is simplistic and naive.

The Lord's first message is that *shrewdness with money can achieve eternal goals*. "Use worldly wealth to gain friends for yourselves." "Worldly wealth" weakens Jesus' phrase, which should be translated "the mammon of unrighteousness." *Mammon* is an interesting term that includes not only money but also possessions. The Lord makes it clear that mammon has enormous power. It is not simply neutral. When it is not placed under the authority of Christ, it becomes a rival god and leads to evil. Thus, it is not simply "worldly wealth" but "unrighteous mammon."

The Lord calls us to recognize the limits of wealth. "So that when it is gone" means literally "when it fails," a reference to death, not debt. As Paul reminds us, "we brought nothing into the world, and we can take nothing out of it" (1 Tim. 6:7). Shrewdness forces us to recognize that money is powerful but limited, temporary, and temporal. Part of its character is that it will always fail. As Bernard of Clairvaux wrote centuries ago, "Money no more satisfies the hunger of the mind than air supplies the body's need for bread." Certainly that is true at the time of death. No one takes it with him.

Shrewdness with money also focuses on how it can be used for eternal purposes. "Gain friends . . . so that . . . you will be welcomed [by them] into eternal dwellings." Every believer will be welcomed into heaven; not all will have the same number of friends to welcome them.

When our money is used to meet the needs of fellow believers and when money is used to spread the gospel, we can be sure that there are eternal consequences. Our gracious Father will reveal to our fellow-saints how our use of money was instrumental in their conversion or in the meeting of their needs. Few experiences are as satisfying as to visit an area where you once lived and ministered and to have people line up to tell you of your influence in their lives, much of it totally unguessed or unrecognized. Imagine that kind of reception in heaven!

The Lord calls us to use money shrewdly for eternal reasons. Yet statistics tell us that as the rate of disposable income, adjusted for inflation, increased 31 percent among members of 31 Protestant denominations between 1968 and 1985, only two percent of that disposable income was given to churches and Christian organizations (*Chicago Tribune*, July 31, 1988). In other words, 98 percent of the increase went to support people's lifestyles. In a world of escalating needs and exciting opportunities, this is hardly shrewdness with money. Believers also need to *live* shrewdly—to strategize, plan, and dream, to use ingenuity and creativity. Radical times require radical solutions, as the dishonest manager illustrates. The Lord is not calling us to business as usual. How can I maximize my money for eternity—this is the question of the shrewd disciple. We must be careful not to spend or give carelessly, sentimentally, or impulsively. The Lord calls us to be hard-nosed, clear-eyed, forward-looking, astute people.

Second, not only can shrewdness with money achieve eternal goals, *stewardship of money has eternal consequences*, as verses 10–12 indicate. The principles of stewardship are very simple. First is the main requirement: "It is required that those who have been given a trust must prove faithful" (1 Cor. 4:2). Second is the reward, explained here by the Lord: "Whoever can be trusted with very little can also be trusted with much, and whoever is dishonest with very little will also be dishonest with much." Little things are the school of life. As the great missionary Hudson Taylor once observed, "A little thing is a little thing; but faithfulness in a little thing is a great thing."

Faithfulness with money is primarily an issue of character. A modern biographer explained with a very perceptive comment why he was adding yet another biography to the literature about the Duke of Wellington: "I had an advantage over earlier biographers. I found an old account ledger that showed how the Duke spent his money. It was a far better clue to what he thought was really important than the reading of his letters or speeches." This is even more true of the account of a disciple.

Shrewdness causes us to view "mammon" in a very interesting way. The parallelism of verses 10–12 equates "very little" (8:10), "worldly wealth" (8:11), and "someone else's property" (8:12). At the same time it equates "much" (8:10), "true riches" (8:11), and "property of your own" (8:12). Present wealth, says the Lord, is really a very little thing. In fact, it is not ours at all. We are stewards, not owners. If we use our present possessions as if they really belong to us, not the Lord, we are acting exactly like the dishonest manager. We are owners of nothing, stewards of everything. What we possess is to be used to further the Master's purposes and goals. The primary value of earthly wealth is that it is a school, training us to handle "true riches," which must refer to the affairs of the kingdom.

Shrewd people, then, use money in the light of eternal consequences. This includes opportunities to serve the Lord Jesus in furthering His purposes on earth as well as the privileges of service we will enjoy in heaven.

Third, the Lord tells us that shrewd disciples recognize that *stewardship of money prevents bondage to money.* "You cannot serve both God and Money." We can serve God with money; we can never serve God and Money. A choice is inescapable. We can have only one master. Jesus wants us to understand that we do not have the option of being the masters of Mammon. We can be stewards of it or we can be servants of it, but those are our only options. Mammon always strives to take the place of God. The Lord is using a vivid personification in this discussion to force us to recognize the absence of middle ground. Either God owns our wealth or it owns us. As Henry Fielding once wrote, "Make money your god and it will plague you like the devil."

We all serve something or someone. There is no partial discipleship to Jesus, and there is no part-time employment by Mammon. We must choose our ultimate loyalty. When we choose the Lord as our sole master, He does not remove our money. In fact, He takes the money and transforms it into an ally. The same dollar that places a bet, pays a prostitute, or purchases cocaine also buys a Bible, digs a well, or supports a missionary. The same dollar the shrewd manager uses to pave his way into a golden future, a shrewd disciple uses to invest in eternal friendships. But the difference is the product of a choice of masters.

How do we get our money? What do we want to get with our money? When do we give our money? Where should we employ our resources? These are the questions a shrewd disciple asks as he emulates his strange "hero," a man who acted decisively with his resources in the present to maximize his opportunities in the future.

The story is told of a man shipwrecked on a lonely, unknown island. To his surprise, he found that he was not alone; a large tribe of people shared his island. To his pleasure, he discovered that they treated him very well. In fact, they placed him on a throne and catered to his every desire. He was delighted but perplexed. Why such royal treatment? As his ability to communicate increased, he discovered that the tribal custom was to choose a king for a year. Then, when his term was finished, he would be transported to a particular island and abandoned.

Delight was now replaced by distress. Then he hit on a shrewd plan. Over the next months he sent members of the tribe to clear and till the other island. He had them build a beautiful house, furnish it, and plant crops. He sent some chosen friends to live there and wait for him. Then, when his time of exile came, he was put in a place carefully prepared and full of friends delighted to receive him.

Disciples are not headed to a desert island but to the Father's home. Yet the preparations we make here follow us there. If we are shrewd, there will be eternal friends and eternal rewards to greet us. Fools serve money and leave it all behind. Shrewd believers serve God and invest in eternity.

# CHAPTER EIGHT

# DETERMINING
# MY DESTINY

Our image of Woody Allen is probably fixed by the type of character he chooses to portray—the born loser, a hapless, bewildered man facing a complex world. But Woody Allen has also been called the most daring and creative moviemaker of our times, a man whose movies reflect important aspects of modern life. There is an autobiographical tone to his work, a wry humor that combines gloom and comedy with a philosophical outlook on life.

Woody Allen claims to be an atheist, yet his work is full of religious themes and he himself seems preoccupied with death. He unburdened himself to one interviewer: "The fundamental thing behind all motivation and activity is the constant struggle against annihilation and against death. It's absolutely stupefying in its terror and it renders anyone's accomplishments meaningless. As Camus said, 'It's not only that *he* dies, or *man* dies, but that you struggle to do a work of art that will last and then realize that *the universe itself* is not going to exist after a period of time.' " The interviewer, touched and surprised by this dark outpouring, asked: "But aren't you happy that you will achieve immortality through achievements?" The idea didn't encourage Allen. "Who cares about achieving immortality through achievements? I'm interested in achieving immortality through not dying."

But that type of immortality is not available to him or anyone else. Although death is a taboo subject in our society, one we do our best to avoid, it just won't go away. The spirituality of the New Age has tried to transmute it by seducing us with promises of reincarnation, astral projection, and soul travel. But all the talk of cosmic energy and psychic adventure cannot change the unalterable: "Man is destined to die once, and after that to face judgment" (Heb. 9:27).

Fascination with life after death has led some to the most amazing (and dangerous) sources of "information." Near-death experiences, ascended masters, spirit guides, and channelers provide pseudo-facts for one cultural stream, while humanists, naturalists, and many philosophers debunk the rationality of life after death. But the only reliable source of information comes from the Lord of life, the Death-Conqueror. By His resurrection, He proved His authority. In His teaching, He gives us certainty. One of His most important lessons is given in the form of a parable, the story of the rich man and Lazarus, where He pulls aside the curtain and gives us insight into ultimate reality.

The parable of the rich man and Lazarus belongs in a special category. Only here is a character in a parable given a name, and some have argued on that basis that this is not a parable at all, but an actual event. That is an unlikely conclusion, since the Lord seems to be using figurative language throughout the story to teach truth. We are not intended to use this parable to develop a geography of heaven and hell or to develop ideas about our form of existence prior to the rapture. The Savior is using earthly language (tongue, thirst, water, etc.) to teach eternal truths about what awaits us on the other side of death.

> "There was a rich man who was dressed in purple and fine linen and lived in luxury every day. At his gate

was laid a beggar named Lazarus,
covered with sores and longing to eat
what fell from the rich man's table.
Even the dogs came and licked his
sores.

"The time came when the beggar
died and the angels carried him to
Abraham's side. The rich man also
died and was buried. In hell, where he
was in torment, he looked up and saw
Abraham far away, with Lazarus by
his side. So he called to him, 'Father
Abraham, have pity on me and send
Lazarus to dip the tip of his finger in
water and cool my tongue, because I
am in agony in this fire.'

"But Abraham replied, 'Son, remember that in your lifetime you
received your good things, while
Lazarus received bad things, but now
he is comforted here and you are in
agony. And besides all this, between
us and you a great chasm has been
fixed, so that those who want to go
from here to you cannot, nor can anyone cross over from there to us.'

"He answered, 'Then I beg you, father, send Lazarus to my father's house, for I have five brothers. Let him warn them, so that they will not also come to this place of torment.'

"Abraham replied, 'They have Moses and the Prophets; let them listen to them.'

" 'No, father Abraham,' he said, 'but if someone from the dead goes to them, they will repent.'

"He said to him, 'If they do not listen to Moses and the Prophets, they will not be convinced even if someone rises from the dead.' "

(Luke 16:19–31)

## A Study in Contrasts: The Earthly Condition of Two Men

When Henry David Thoreau was on his deathbed, he was visited by a minister who urged his dying friend to be ready for death: "Do you know where you're going in the next world?" Thoreau waved him away with the words, "One world at a time." His attitude has caused humanists to uphold him as a man of moral courage, resisting a cowardly flight to religion. He was, in fact, the model of a fool. Imagine a man in Florida boarding a plane to Alaska in mid-winter with no baggage, who answers the question, "Do you know where you're going?" with "One city at a time, my friend." Only a fool fails to plan ahead for the inevitable.

Fools are not always evident as such. The Lord Jesus paints the picture of the rich man so that we see clearly the affluence in which he basked. His clothing was splendid—purple and fine linen were first-century equivalents of silk sheets and designer clothing. His lifestyle was sumptuous; he enjoyed comfortable surroundings, rich food, and self-indulgent luxury. His was the good life, and he was very good at living it.

When most of the world looks at North America, it sees people who resemble this man. There is something both enticing and deceiving about living in prosperity. We can shelter ourselves from the darker realities of life and busy ourselves so that we suppress disturbing questions. As Robert Maynard Hutchins observes, "Our real problems are concealed from us by our current remarkable prosperity, which results in part from our new way of getting rich, which is to buy things from one another that we do not want, at prices we cannot pay, on terms we cannot meet, because of advertising we do not believe" (cited by Donald McCullough in *Waking from the American Dream*, p. 73).

At the rich man's gate was a man at the opposite end of the scale. We have become used to homeless people living on grates outside buildings containing luxurious apartments. Travel in the Third World makes this picture even more vivid. Abject poverty exists side by side with vulgar displays of wealth. It is hard to enjoy a meal in a restaurant when you realize that the person at the door is a guard, posted not to help you in but to keep beggars out. It is even harder when children do get in and stand by your table with hands extended for money or food. I had both of these experiences in a Central American country. This parable depicts the tragic reality of life in many parts of our world.

Lazarus was a beggar. His name was a lofty one, based on the Hebrew name Eleazar, which means "God is my helper." But his situation was pitiful. He was physically ill. The little expression "was laid" indicates that he was disabled and depended on others for movement. His body was covered with ulcerous sores, and these almost certainly made him repulsive to see and disgusting to smell. He was hungry, longing to eat table scraps. In Palestine, people did not use knives and forks to pick up food, but bread. It was often thrown on the floor after use. This is what he longed to eat. Further, he was helpless. The dogs that came to lick his sores were not pet poodles but wild dogs, who only made his condition worse. But he lacked the strength to keep them away. He was the epitome of helplessness and neediness.

A more dramatic contrast cannot be imagined—two men at the opposite poles of affluence and misery. A superficial evaluation pities Lazarus as the loser and condemns the rich man as the villain, a first-century Ebenezer Scrooge ignoring appropriate decencies. Lazarus certainly was a sufferer, and the rich man's inhumanity was wicked. But there is a deeper contrast between the two men, not visible to the human eye and revealed only after death. It has nothing to do with economic status.

## Turning the Tables: The Eternal Condition of Two Men

Lazarus's death probably came as a surprise to no one and was of concern to few. His body's disposal is not described. But what is said would have surprised many of Jesus' hearers. Conventional Jewish wisdom suggested that misery on earth was due to divine disapproval. On those terms, Lazarus would obviously qualify as a man under God's punishment. Instead, we read that "the angels carried him to Abraham's side." There is no parallel to this anywhere else in Scripture, and we shouldn't speculate about the ministry of angels to dead believers. But this passage clearly reveals God's acceptance and approval of Lazarus.

Lazarus's destination is "Abraham's side" (literally, his chest). The chest is spoken of in Scripture as the place of special intimacy, of fellowship and care. John in his gospel loves to describe himself as "the one who had leaned back against Jesus [literally, "upon His chest"] at the supper" (John 21:20). Abraham was the great man of faith, the father of the faithful, God's friend. So the expression is a vivid way of saying that Lazarus is exalted to a position of the highest honor and intimacy in the heavenly fellowship of the saints. No greater reversal of fortunes can be imagined. Lazarus has been transported from the gutter to heaven's head table.

Marvelous as this description is, it pales alongside later revelations about the destiny of believers. We do not depart to be with Abraham and the righteous saints, but to be with the Lord Jesus (Phil. 1:23). We do not enter the home of Abraham, but rather are "at home with the Lord" (2 Cor. 5:8) in the Father's house (John 14:2). We share the very highest place a creature can experience.

But why is Lazarus welcomed into heaven? Some have suggested that it was simply because he was poor. But saying that mere poverty qualifies for heaven denies everything else taught in the Bible about the way of salvation. At this point in the story, we must wait for an explanation.

The rich man also dies. We can imagine an expensive and elaborate funeral, fitting to a man of his wealth and status. In death as in life, his body is well cared for. But he dies as he lived, with no provision for his soul. Money and luxury cannot follow him past the grave. No angels carry him to Abraham's side. Rather, we read, he finds himself "in hell, where he was in torment."

In the Old Testament, we read about Sheol, the place of the dead, the grave. All people go to the grave. But what lies beyond the burial of the body? The New Testament speaks of hell or Hades, a place where no believer goes. In the full teaching of God's Word, we learn that Hades is the immediate destination of all unbelievers, prior to their final arraignment at God's great white throne, which is followed by their eternal confinement in the lake of fire (Rev. 20:11–15).

The rich man's experience sets before us three terrifying facts. First, *Hades is real*. The language may be symbolic (fire, tongue, water), but the experience is real. The Lord Jesus, more than anyone else in Scripture, teaches about eternal punishment and eternal fire. Second, *Hades is terrible*. The rich man is not annihilated or unconscious. He is in "torment" (16:23, 28) and "in agony" (16:24–25). That is expressed in psychological, physical, and spiritual terms. A great, unbridgeable chasm is fixed, and the rich man is fully aware of what Lazarus enjoys that he does not. At the same time, he is fully aware that he deserves what he is receiving.

He doesn't ask Abraham for release from torment, but for relief within it. Third, *Hades is final*. That is to say, the rich man's destiny is unchangeable. The great chasm is fixed "so that those who want to go from here to you cannot, nor can anyone cross over from there to us." There is no graduation or parole from Hades. There is no purgatory, no suspended sentence, no conditional immortality. Separation from God is eternal.

We may raise questions about the meaning of some of the story's details. For example, I do not think we are to conclude that people in heaven continually witness the torments of hell or that conversations are held back and forth. But our questions must not blur the clear and awful message coming from the lips of the Incarnation of eternal love. Hell is an awful, awesome, eternal reality, indescribably fearful to consider. And human beings will be there because of choices made in this present life. That thought should bring tears to our eyes and a godly fear to our hearts that causes us to make sure of our own destiny, and that gives urgency to our message as we share the gospel.

But why did Lazarus go to Abraham's side, while the rich man found himself in hell? If Lazarus did not qualify for heaven due to his poverty, did the rich man qualify for hell because of his wealth? If so, why is Abraham, one of the wealthiest men of his day, in heaven? We need to listen carefully to the discussion between Abraham and the rich man, not only to answer these all-important questions but to hear the Lord's message.

## Hearing the Scriptures: The Dividing Line

The rich man has been denied even a temporary alleviation of his distress. He has also been told that his condition is unchangeable. But he has one more request: "I beg you, father, send Lazarus to my father's house, for I have five brothers. Let him warn them, so that they will not also come to this place of torment." The rich man is perceptive enough to realize that his brothers are on a course of life that will bring them to Hades. They need to be warned, and they need to repent. Surely a message from a resurrected Lazarus would have the desired effect.

If we read the request as a man's loving concern for his doomed brothers, we will miss

the point and misrepresent hell. Implicit in the
request is an attack on God himself: "I didn't
have a fair chance. God could have done
more. If He had communicated more clearly
or attracted my attention more dramatically, I
would have repented. And so will my brothers.
My destiny is God's fault, not mine."

There are millions who are imitators of
the rich man at this point. "I'll believe, if God
makes it clear enough. If I don't believe, that's
God's fault." Such an attitude betrays profound
ignorance about ourselves and deep blasphemy
against God. In one of his movies, Woody Allen
has his character say to his beloved Laura, "If
only God would speak to me—just once. If he
would only cough. If I could just see a miracle.
If I could see a burning bush or the seas part.
Or my uncle Sasha pick up the check." The
humor is typical of Allen; so is the unbelief.
God has spoken in His creation. He has spoken
in history. He has spoken in His Word. Above
all, He has spoken in His Son, and no one is
without responsibility or has a valid excuse.

Abraham will not entertain this slander on
God for even a moment: "They have Moses
and the Prophets; let them listen to them." God
needs to do nothing greater than He has done

in giving men written Scripture. His Word is clear, sufficient, and powerful. The brothers' need is not to hear a messenger risen from the grave, but to listen to the Word of God given from heaven. They do not require an added experience to validate Scripture or to demonstrate God's veracity. They need to listen to the Word.

The rich man is not satisfied: "No, father Abraham, but if someone from the dead goes to them, they will repent." A voice from the grave will make all the difference. It is important to note how the issue has crystallized. The rich man's presence in hell has nothing to do with his possession of wealth, or his self-indulgent use of it. He has callously disregarded Lazarus's need and has lived in rebellion against the clear command of Scripture, given in Isaiah 58:6–7:

> "Is not this the kind of fasting I have chosen: to loose the chains of injustice and untie the cords of the yoke, to set the oppressed free and break every yoke? Is it not to share your food with the hungry and to provide the poor wanderer with shelter—when you see the naked, to clothe him, and

not to turn away from your own flesh
and blood?"

His sin is clear. But ultimately the rich man
is in hell because he has not listened to the
Word of God and repented before it. He has
not believed God's truth. It is not wealth that
excludes from heaven, but unbelief. And,
although we are not explicitly told so here, it is
not Lazarus's poverty that has qualified him for
"Abraham's side." The clear, consistent witness
of Scripture is that salvation is by faith alone.
The words the Lord puts in Abraham's
mouth to conclude the parable are extremely
important. "If they do not listen to Moses and
the Prophets, they will not be convinced even if
someone rises from the dead." People who are
not changed by Scripture will not be changed
by a miracle. That is why Abraham refuses the
request—not because he does not care about
the fate of the rich man's brothers, but because
the request is futile. It does not address the
need. Miracles do not melt stony hearts. This
fact is demonstrated consistently through the
Scriptures.

- At the Exodus, Israel is miraculously
  delivered from Egypt, sees God's power in

the desert, and yet persists in unbelief, so that God asks, "How long will they refuse to believe in me, in spite of all the miraculous signs I have performed among them?" (Num. 14:11).

- Elijah and Elisha perform undeniable and evident miracles, yet the northern kingdom persists in its rebellion, resulting in God's exile of the nation (cf. 1 Kings 18:16–46; 2 Kings 2:19–22).
- The Lord's miracles are met by unbelief and blasphemous denial of who He is (e.g., Matt. 11:20–24).
- The raising of Lazarus from the dead results in some believing (John 11:45), but only intensifies the unbelief and antagonism of the Jewish leaders (John 11:46–53; 12:10–11).
- When the Jewish leaders admit that the apostles "have done an outstanding miracle" (Acts 4:16), they intensify their persecution.
- The empty tomb does not lead the unbelieving to come in faith, but to concoct a false story, to explain away the resurrection of the Lord Jesus (Matt. 28:11–15).

All this confirms the Lord's words. The primary use of miracles in Scripture was not to *convince* people of the truth by replacing the Bible, but rather to *confirm* the truth of Scripture. People are responsible for hearing and repenting before what God has said in the Word. The Lord's story warns us about two destinies—heaven and hell. It also reminds us of the one great, inescapable responsibility—to take God at His word.

The parable of the rich man and Lazarus forces us to think seriously about our eternal destiny. There is no immortality that comes by "not dying." Rich or poor, powerful or powerless, healthy or ill, we will all face not only death but eternal destiny. The grave works no miracles. Our present relation to God through His Word determines our eternal relationship with Him.

This parable also clarifies our present responsibility if we are believers. It is to make it clear to all that God has spoken in His Word and calls everyone to hear and repent. Some Christians have suggested that true evangelism is "power evangelism," in which resistance to the gospel is overcome by the demonstration of God's power in supernatural events. This, we are told, makes "receptivity to Christ's claims very high." In fact, it has even been suggested that people who do not experience such power are less likely not only to believe but to move on to a mature faith. But the Lord's words suggest something very different. True power evangelism involves not the doing of miracles but the proclamation of God's truth in Scripture, which is able to make people "wise for salvation through faith in Christ Jesus" (2 Tim. 3:15). The power that is needed is the power of Spirit-filled people sharing the Spirit-given truths of Scripture. God's Word is sufficient not only to meet believers' needs, but also to meet the needs of unbelievers. As we are confident in the inherent truth and power of Scripture, we will bring to the "rich men" of our time that which they need most, and to the hurting Lazaruses that which will help them longest. We must not leave the Lazaruses of our time needy and helpless at the gate, but, in our concern to minister to their desperate present needs, we must not neglect their deepest, eternal needs.

# CHAPTER NINE

# ASKING MY FATHER

Frequent fliers treat the pre-flight safety announcements the way many people treat evangelists. They are convinced that, while the information may be true, it's probably unnecessary, and, if it ever does become vital, either further instruction will be given or common sense will pull them through. I can identify. I've flown hundreds of thousands of miles, and the only time I've ever seen an oxygen mask was during the pre-flight ritual. I would be happy if one never appeared, but if it does, I will grab it quickly and use it gratefully.

I must admit that I often view prayer in that way—as a spiritual oxygen mask important in times of emergency or special need. Yet, if I take the Lord Jesus seriously, I know that prayer is more like oxygen than an oxygen mask. That is, it is a constant essential of life. As Martin Luther observed, "To be a Christian without prayer is no more possible than to be alive without breathing." Prayer is more than a privilege; it is a necessity, an indispensable part of our walk with God.

But honesty forces me to admit that prayer is often a problem. It is easier to preach about prayer than to pray. Most of the difficulty is not intellectual, although there are some aspects of it that are hard to understand. But the problem seems to lie at a deeper, more mysterious level. What should I pray about and how should I do it? Am I doing it right? If prayer is so great, why does it feel like a burden or a duty, or worse, like religious play-acting? Does God really hear and answer me?

Prayer was a subject that was on the Lord's mind constantly. He prayed, and He taught His disciples about prayer. But it was not simply a spiritual discipline for Him. He did not focus on prayer so much as on His Father. This in itself is of great importance. Most of our problems with prayer are due to our misconceptions about God. If we understood Him better, we would both pray more and enjoy it more. So Jesus does not give His people a praying technique so much as an appreciation of the recipient of prayer. One place we encounter that teaching is in the parable of the midnight caller found in

Luke 11:5–8. But before Christ tells His story, He sets out a pattern to guide us in prayer.

## Going to the Expert: The Pattern of Prayer (Luke 11:1–4)

> One day Jesus was praying in a certain place. When he finished, one of his disciples said to him, "Lord, teach us to pray, just as John taught his disciples." He said to them, "When you pray, say: 'Father, hallowed be your name, your kingdom come. Give us each day our daily bread. Forgive us our sins, for we also forgive everyone who sins against us. And lead us not into temptation.' "

Suppose you want to develop a skill—driving a car, playing golf or using a computer. To whom do you go? A wise person doesn't turn to a willing friend but to a qualified expert. The expert on prayer is obviously the Lord Jesus. We would make a mistake if we read the statement "One day Jesus was praying in a certain place" as describing an unusual event. Luke makes very clear that prayer was a normal activity for the Lord. "Jesus often withdrew to lonely places and prayed" (Luke 5:16). At least seven times, Luke specifically records that Jesus prayed, and prayer precedes every significant event in His life—His baptism (3:21), His choosing of the disciples (6:12), Peter's confession of faith (9:18), the transfiguration (9:28–29), and the crucifixion (Gethsemane, 22:39–46). If the God-man chose to pray constantly and consistently, how much more should we?

The disciples not only recognized the priority of prayer in their Lord's life, they were impressed by what they saw. They must have sensed that it was, in some way, the secret of His life, and that He was strong at a place where they were weak. "Lord, teach us to pray" is the only record in Scripture of them asking Him to teach them anything.

I have been intrigued by the way you can discover something about people's spiritual roots by listening to them pray. Some groups have their own characteristics—a certain kind of language or particular phrases or interjections ("Thank you, Jesus," "Amen," "Uh-huh"). Praying across denominational lines can be a fascinating cross-cultural experience! Perhaps the disciples have something similar in mind when they add, "just as John taught his disciples." Jewish groups had distinctive corporate prayers and prayer styles, and John had apparently given his followers a recognizable pattern. Jesus' disciples want a Jesus-style prayer. But they want more than a prayer to recite. Their request is not "Teach us a prayer," but "Teach us to pray."

That is what Jesus does in the familiar words of the Lord's Prayer. We misread His intention if we just hear Him giving us a liturgical prayer. A simple comparison of Luke's record of the Lord's Prayer with the variation given in Matthew 6:9–13 shows that, even in its earliest forms, it was not a rote prayer but a model prayer. That is, while it is not wrong to recite the prayer, it is more important to understand its principles. The rest of the New Testament never tells of Christians using these precise words; it does tell of believers praying based on their example.

An extensive exposition of this marvelous model is beyond our present purpose. But, while much more could be said, we must at least observe three great prayer principles found here.

1. *Prayer is to the Father.* Bound up in the simple address "Father" is the heart of all that the Lord Jesus came to do. Old Testament believers are never said to address God in this way. Jewish prayers began, "Lord God of Abraham, God of Isaac, God of Jacob, God most high, creator of heaven and earth, our shield and the shield of our fathers!" But from the time of our Lord's earthly life and His death upon the cross, believers have been able to come as children and cry out "Father!" This makes clear the simplicity and brevity of true prayer; it is not the heaping up of elaborate and ornate language. Christian prayer is the language of intimacy, the loving conversation of a Father and His child. Prayer's central purpose is not to transfer information. After all, what can you tell an all-knowing God that He does not already know? Rather, it is to deepen the relationship we have with one who is all that a father could ever be and much more.

2. *Prayer is about the Father's glory.* "Hallowed be your name" is a plea that God's reputation will be honored by men. "Your kingdom come" anticipates that our Lord's reign will be established on the earth. Ultimately, this looks forward to the Lord's return in His

kingdom glory, and it also reminds us that, as His kingdom people, we can live under His authority now and extend His rule by sharing the gospel. What we must not miss is that, in prayer, God's glory and God's program take precedence over all else. We pervert prayer if we make it primarily about getting our needs met, rather than desiring that our Father be honored and obeyed properly.

3. *Prayer is about our needs.* To say that prayer is primarily God-centered is not to say that petition is wrong. On the contrary, there are no concerns that the Father does not want us to bring to Him. "Daily bread" represents every need related to our physical existence. Bread is a necessity, not a luxury; an essential, not just a desire. We come for such needs, just as we also come asking, "forgive us our sins"—a sobering admission that we are sinful, failing people who need help in our relationship with God and with others. And we are vulnerable people who are drawn to sin the way a moth is drawn to the flame. "Lead us not into temptation" reminds us of our continuing moral needs, which are due to the power of sin within us and Satan outside us.

Having given the disciples a pattern of prayer, the Lord continues His instruction by telling a story. The focus of the story is important, because it forces us to think deeply about the one to whom our prayer is made.

## Calling at Midnight: The Parable of Prayer

> Then he said to them, "Suppose one of you has a friend, and he goes to him at midnight and says, 'Friend, lend me three loaves of bread, because a friend of mine on a journey has come to me, and I have nothing to set before him.'
>
> "Then the one inside answers, 'Don't bother me. The door is already locked, and my children are with me in bed. I can't get up and give you anything.' I tell you, though he will not get up and give him the bread because he is his friend, yet because of the man's boldness he will get up and give him as much as he needs."
>
> (Luke 11:5–8)

"Midnight Caller" is a title familiar to television viewers. But the Lord's story about a midnight caller is directed to a very different end. Its circumstances would not be unusual to Jesus' audience. Summer days in Palestine are almost as brutally hot as they are in my home state, Texas. Even today, with the luxury of air-conditioned cars, wise travelers start early to avoid the intense heat. In ancient Judea the more common solution was to travel in the early evening. Probably the man in the story did the same but encountered some unexpected delays. His journey took longer than planned, so he arrived later than intended. Inns were either not available or very undesirable, so he arrived unexpectedly at the home of his friend. His unprepared host now faced a dilemma. His guest was hungry after a long journey, and custom made it the host's duty to provide a meal. Not to do so would have brought disgrace not only on the man but on the entire village. But there were no refrigerators or local convenience stores, and his cupboards were empty. Desperate, he turned to his only alternative—a friend who could supply what he needed. Far past bedtime, he went to his neighbor and appealed for help: "Friend, lend

me what I need. I can't feed my guest!" It
is helpful to recognize that this man wasn't
acting selfishly; he was driven by a sense of his
guest's need. He would never have done this if
he had merely been hungry and wanted a late
night snack.

To appreciate the Lord's story, we need to
picture a one-room peasant's home, such as is
still found widely in most Third World countries.
The whole family would have slept in that
room, usually on mats on the floor. When the
door was bolted shut, no one could get up to
open it without awakening everyone. In such
an arrangement, to say "I can't get up to give
you anything" is really to say "I won't do it." The
neighbor's reluctance is understandable; his
refusal is against everything his culture values.

But, the Lord assures us, he will respond.
Although friendship may not rouse him from his
bed, something else will. "I tell you, though he
will not get up and give him the bread because
he is his friend, yet because of the man's
boldness, he will get up and give him as much
as he needs." The word translated "the man's
boldness" has been a puzzle to translators. It
is used only once in the New Testament and
basically means "shamelessness." Most often,

it has been translated "persistence"—the man will act to get rid of this nuisance caller. While that may be true, it isn't quite the sense of the Greek word. Others have thought that it refers to the sense of shame the neighbor would feel. He would act to protect his honor and his reputation in the community. True as it may be, that also doesn't seem to be the precise meaning the Lord intended. The word means "boldness, audacity, shamelessness." Humans respond to audacious requests. When a fearful mother phones a doctor friend at 2:00 a.m., the doctor pays attention not just to the request but to the timing of it. Obviously she believes that this call is important. Were a neighbor to phone after midnight with a request, I would realize that this was not a casual conversation. The boldness reveals the importance. And almost always, such late requests are not selfish or trivial. I'm not going to knock on my neighbor's door at 3:00 a.m. to borrow a cup of sugar!

But how are we to understand this of prayer? Is God like a sleepy neighbor who is irritated when I come to Him at an inconvenient time with a deep need? Does He have to be badgered or shamed into responding? Has He "gone to bed?" or is He temporarily "out of touch"? Exactly the opposite is true. He is not a sleepy friend but a loving Father. If a drowsy neighbor will respond to boldness when my need is real and urgent, how much more will my unwearied Father? If an emergency arises in my child's life at an unearthly hour, I may not be thrilled when I get the call, but I want to get it and to do all I can to help. My God is all the more eager to help and all the more anxious to respond to my deep need.

The parable then is not a parable of comparison but of contrast. The Lord is not like the sleepy neighbor at all. He does not need to be shamed or cajoled into acting. He is sure to hear and quick to answer. The Lord doesn't make that point explicitly. But in the exhortations to prayer that follow, He invites us to come boldly and confidently to the Father.

## Knocking at the Door: Principles of Prayer

"So I say to you: Ask and it will be given to you; seek and you will find; knock and the door will be opened to you. For everyone who asks receives; he who seeks finds; and to him who knocks, the door will be opened.

"Which of you fathers, if your son
asks for a fish, will give him a snake
instead? Or if he asks for an egg,
will give him a scorpion? If you then,
though you are evil, know how to give
good gifts to your children, how much
more will your Father in heaven give
the Holy Spirit to those who ask him!"

(Luke 11:9–13)

The first thing the Lord sets before us is *the principle of persistence*. The words themselves, "ask . . . seek . . . knock," suggest this, and each of them occurs in the present tense in the Greek language. This indicates a continuing action: "Keep on asking," which implies a faith that makes requests; "keep on seeking," which indicates a sincerity that is more than casual; "keep on knocking," which shows that initial barriers are not to be seen as final refusals.

The Lord doesn't tell us for what we are to ask, seek, or knock. But He does tell us that we are to come to the Father, convinced that He is committed to meet our needs. We do not need to nag Him or pester Him, but we do need to persist. The Lord often uses delay to deepen our dependence upon Him or to refine our understanding of what we need from Him. Prayer involves seeing ourselves as needy people without the resources to meet our needs. We will not continue to ask if we do not really feel a need or if we believe we can do it on our own. But if we recognize that God alone can supply what we lack, we will seek, ask, and knock persistently. However, the basis of prayer is not our persistence but the character of our God. We keep praying because we are convinced that we have a good and loving Father who has committed himself to answer us.

There is, however, a problem with the glorious promise that "everyone who asks receives; he who seeks finds; and to him who knocks, the door will be opened." Does this mean I receive whatever I ask for? If so, the promise has proven untrue. Almost all of us can describe unanswered prayers. But, even more, the promise would be dangerous. Some of the things I have prayed for, sure that I needed them at the time, seem foolish or even harmful in retrospect. And such a concept would reduce God to a servant, whose role is to cater to the whims of His spoiled children. I do not want God to give me what I want; I trust Him to give me what I need. The truth is, He is infinitely wiser than I am. If we always get what we ask for, I for one will cease to pray.

That is why the Lord also gives us the principle of confidence. Simply put, if we trust human fathers, sinful as they are, to act in our best interests, how much more can we have confidence in our perfect heavenly Father? The parable of the midnight caller builds on the contrast between the sleepy friend and the unwearied friend. The picture the Lord gives in verses 11–13 builds from the lesser to the greater, from earthly fathers to the heavenly Father.

No human father is perfect. All of us are sinful and selfish, and even the best of us have some harmful effects upon our children. But generally, our selfishness is combined with a loving concern for them. When our children ask for what they need (a fish or an egg), we do not mock their requests or give them something destructive and harmful (a snake or a scorpion). We try to give them what they need and, if possible, to give them what they want. We know how to give good gifts to our children, and we enjoy doing it. What father hasn't thrilled to the excited appreciation of a satisfied child?

"How much more will your Father in heaven give . . . to those who ask Him?" As a Father, He will do no less than an earthly father. He delights to respond to His children's needs. And as a perfect Father, He will do much more than any human father. I am able to hear my children's requests; often I am not wise enough to discern their needs. I worry when I say yes that my affirmation may be harmful. Am I spoiling my child? I sometimes worry when I say no that my denial is selfish or shortsighted. I do the best I can, but sometimes my best just isn't good enough. My Father in heaven knows no such limits. He never gives foolishly or haphazardly. He never withholds selfishly or because He lacks resources. He never says yes because He is insecure and wants to "buy" my love. He never says no because He is distracted, exhausted, or irritable. I can go to Him with unlimited confidence that He is Lord. He will never give me what is contrary to my good or His glory.

But what will He give me? As Matthew records these words, the promise is, He will "give good gifts to those who ask him!" (Matt. 7:11). What a great assurance! But as Luke records the words, the Lord was more specific on another occasion. The promise in Luke is that He will "give the Holy Spirit to those who ask him!" The good gift the Father is ready to give is His Holy Spirit. He is the bread and food for which we are to ask, seek, and knock. He is the bread and food we are to ask for in other's lives, as the parable of the midnight caller suggests.

What are we to make of this statement? We know that the Holy Spirit does not come by invitation but by salvation. " 'If anyone is thirsty, let him come to me and drink. Whoever believes in me, as the Scripture has said, streams of living water will flow from within him.' By this he meant the Spirit, whom those who believed in him were later to receive" (John 7:37–39). Since the day of Pentecost this promise has instantaneously been fulfilled in the life of everyone who trusts in the Lord Jesus Christ. As God's children, we do not ask to receive the Spirit, as if we do not possess Him in our lives. He is God's good gift to every believer.

It is tempting, then, to dismiss the promise in verse 13 as referring to another time and place. After all, the Lord was speaking prior to Pentecost. His words must apply to that era. But in *no* period of God's program was the Holy

Spirit received by asking for Him. What can He mean? Two passages in Ephesians give us a clue. Paul prays that the glorious Father "may give you the Spirit of wisdom and revelation, so that you may know Him better" (Eph. 1:17). He has already made it clear that believers are sealed and indwelt by the Spirit (Eph. 1:13–14), but this prayer is for a specific ministry of God's Spirit to us, beyond His indwelling. Paul prays, as well, in Ephesians 3:16, that "He may strengthen you with power through his Spirit in your inner being." He is asking that the indwelling Spirit minister in a particular way in the lives of God's children.

This teaches us another fundamental truth about prayer, the *principle of assistance*. The gift for which we should be praying and the gift the Father delights to give is His Holy Spirit, who ministers to the deepest needs of our hearts. This is not to deny what the Lord's Prayer has already taught us, that we are to bring our "daily bread" needs to Him. But, too often, the things we set our hearts on in prayer are the secondary things. What we most need to seek, knock, and ask for are those things that only God the Spirit can do for us.

So the Lord has taught us how to pray. We are to pray trustingly, confident that a loving Father hears, cares, and responds. We are to pray persistently and audaciously, coming boldly to our God. We are to pray intimately, knowing that when we knock, it is our Father who will open the door. We are to pray wisely. That is to say, we need to recognize that, while we desire God's gifts, what we really need is God himself, made real to us through His indwelling Spirit.

So how do you see prayer—as an oxygen mask or as oxygen? Many of us are spiritual asthmatics, wheezing our way through life, gasping for air because our spiritual lives have been constricted by prayerlessness. When we pray, we admit that we cannot do it on our own, that we need our Father. And when we pray, we also experience our Father, enjoying His presence and receiving His answers. A believer lives by knowing and asking the Father.

# CHAPTER TEN

# REACHING GOD'S EAR

Shortly after the Duke of Wellington led his troops to victory in the decisive battle against Napoleon and the French at Waterloo, he was asked to compare the courage of the two armies. "My soldiers were not braver than the enemy!" he observed. "But they were brave five minutes longer."

In almost any area of life, staying power is indispensable for success. The most gifted individual in the world will accomplish very little if he quits under pressure, or if the mood to endure only hits every now and then. The brilliance of Wayne Gretzky or Joe Montana isn't the product of impulse but a product crafted in the furnace of pain and on the anvil of repetitious practice. William Carey became the founder of modern missions, a man whose life had an impact upon England, India, and the worldwide Christian community. A cobbler with little formal education, he determined on the seemingly impossible task of going to India to translate the Scriptures. Getting there was hard enough. Staying there was tougher; year after year he experienced overwhelming obstacles and intractable problems. But at the end of his life, having established a mission station, started churches, translated the Scriptures, and set in motion the modern missionary movement, he was asked how, in the midst of so much adversity and misunderstanding, he could accomplish so much. "I can plod," he replied. "I can persevere in any definite pursuit. To this I owe everything. Few people know what may be done till they try and persevere in what they undertake."

Perseverance isn't a very romantic concept. We would rather admire the exploit than examine the endurance that made it possible. We want to believe that if something is really good, it is effortless. But we know better. Endurance is essential. To quote that noted football philosopher Vince Lombardi, "When the going gets tough, the tough get going." But that begs the question. How do you get tough? Where do endurance and staying power come from, especially in the spiritual realm, which calls for a special kind of toughness?

We live in a difficult world that is not friendly to the life of a disciple. The Lord was well aware of this, and one of His great concerns was to prepare His followers for life in this hostile world. His people can be resilient and spiritually tough. However, that resilience is not the product of determination but of prayer. He has directed us in the parable of the midnight caller to the boldness that should characterize our prayer. In the parable of the unjust judge, found in Luke 18:1–8, we are directed to the perseverance that is produced by persistence in prayer.

## The Necessity of Persistent Prayer

> Then Jesus told his disciples a parable to show them that they should always pray and not give up.
>
> (Luke 18:1)

Luke 18:1 actually records for us the continuation and completion of a conversation. The original Greek text makes that clear by saying, "Now he was telling *them* a parable. . . ." The episode began in 17:20 with a question from the Pharisees about "when the kingdom of God would come." This was a constant concern for Jews of all theological backgrounds, and

the Lord himself had announced that the
kingdom was at hand, and even that "the
kingdom of God has come to you" (11:20).
His answer to the Pharisees described the
way in which the kingdom was present: "The
kingdom of God does not come with your
careful observation, nor will people say, 'Here
it is,' or 'There it is,' because the kingdom of
God is within you" (17:20–21). The translation
"within" is unfortunate. These Pharisees were
unbelievers. How could the kingdom be within
them? Nowhere in the Gospels is the kingdom
spoken of as an internalized spiritual reign of
Christ within people's hearts. The Greek term is
accurately and more appropriately translated,
"in your midst." The kingdom was present in the
person of the King. In His presence, it was there
in first-century Judea.

But such a presence of the kingdom was
very different from what the Old Testament had
led people to expect, so the Lord turned to His
disciples to clarify for them the coming, that
is, the display, of the kingdom in its full power
and glory. There will be a day when "the Son
of Man is revealed" (17:30)—when, "in his day,"
He "flashes and lights up the sky from one end
to the other" (17:24). That day will be a time

when evil is destroyed (17:27, 29). But prior to that time, evil will flourish, and God's people will know suffering.

How will disciples make it through those times of distress, when even the Son of Man "must suffer many things and be rejected by this generation" (17:25) and when God's chosen ones "cry . . . out to him day and night" (18:7)? How do we make it through times that are a challenge to faith (18:8)? These are the unasked questions that lie behind the statement that "they should always pray and not give up" (18:1). The word "give up" describes the temptation to quit in despair when we are tired. Giving up is motivated by weariness that comes from living in a sinful, hostile world, feeling worn out by injustice, mistreatment, misunderstanding, and personal failure.

How do we keep going when we feel like bailing out? The cost of being a disciple tempts us to lose heart. Swimming against the current is tiring—why not go with the flow? It is easier to float than to fight. How tempting it is to drift with the current morally, socially, ethically, or spiritually! How do the tough keep going—by determination or positive thinking or strategic retreat from the world?

The Lord's formula is clear and simple:
"They should always pray and not give up." The
antidote to despair is not determination but
dependence, not positive thinking but prayer.
And "should always pray" doesn't say it quite
strongly enough. Prayer is not something we
are permitted to do if we please. The word
should be translated "must": "they must always
pray and not give up." Prayer is what we are
commanded to do as God's will. It is the only
sure basis of perseverance, since it is the
means God uses to accomplish His will in our
lives.

Furthermore, we must not only pray, we
must always pray. "Pray continually" (1 Thes.
5:17). "Pray in the Spirit on all occasions with
all kinds of prayers and requests" (Eph. 6:18).
Does that mean our time must be spent on
nothing but prayer? No, but it does mean that
we must do nothing without prayer. The rabbis
warned the Jewish people against wearying
God with incessant prayer and indicated that
prayers should be said only three times a day,
although there were exceptions. Islam also calls
its adherents to their prayer mats five times a
day. In contrast, the Lord Jesus calls us not
to say prayers but to pray continually. God's

misunderstood and suffering people have one constant resource in a world that is not conducive to faith, and that resource is prayer. If we do not pray, we will grow weary and "fall into temptation" (Luke 22:40).

The Lord's coming kingdom is a glorious hope. But although I am a citizen of the kingdom, I live in the world before the kingdom has been established in power. If I am to persevere, to live with confidence and poise, there is only one solution. I must always pray. To stop praying is to start growing weary. And to encourage us in our prayer the Lord tells a rather startling parable.

## The Parable of Persistent Prayer

> He said: "In a certain town there was a judge who neither feared God nor cared about men. And there was a widow in that town who kept coming to him with the plea, 'Grant me justice against my adversary.'
>
> "For some time he refused. But finally he said to himself, 'Even though I don't fear God or care about men, yet because this widow keeps

bothering me, I will see that she gets
justice, so that she won't eventually
wear me out with her coming!' "

(Luke 18:2–5)

The story takes us into the legal system of the
Lord's time and introduces us to two people
at opposite ends of the legal spectrum. The
judge is the epitome of power. His position
has invested him with authority, and within
his own sphere he can act with little fear
of opposition. His sense of his own power
is expressed succinctly: he "neither feared
God nor cared about people." He is a hard-
bitten man of the world. He has no sense of
personal accountability to God or submission
to divine law. And his heart is never troubled
by sensitivity to people. He cannot be reached
on the grounds of either conscience or
compassion. He does whatever he likes, and is
controlled only by his own inclinations.
The widow represents the depth of
helplessness and weakness. As a woman in a
chauvinistic society, she has almost no political
clout. As a widow in that time, she almost
certainly knows dire poverty. The death of her
husband has left her without an advocate or a

protector, and some unscrupulous individual
has exploited her weakness. Justice may be on
her side, but she has no weapons with which to
fight. She is helpless before an indifferent judge.
Or so it seems. Her every appeal is met by
contemptuous silence. Jewish legal custom,
based on the Old Testament, called for priority
to be given to the legal needs of widows and
orphans. But precedent has no power over such
a man. "For some time he refused." Although
he continues to refuse, she continues to come.
Persistence is her only resource, and finally
she strikes pay dirt. The judge concludes, in
effect, "I don't care about God's law or people's
opinions. But this woman is wearing me out. If
I give her what she wants, then she'll leave me
alone." The judge is motivated entirely by self-
interest. He has no interest in either justice or
the woman's rights. Yet he acts on her behalf.
So a powerless woman with no weapon but
persistence receives her rights from an evil
judge.

The story is a startling one. How can the
Lord tell such a story about prayer? Is prayer
nagging God? Are we to think of God as a
selfish judge who needs to be manipulated and
pestered into doing the right thing? None of us

would dare make such a comparison. What can the Lord mean? He gives us some insight by the words that follow the parable.

## The Pattern of Persistent Prayer

> And the Lord said, "Listen to what the unjust judge says. And will not God bring about justice for his chosen ones, who cry out to him day and night? Will he keep putting them off? I tell you, he will see that they get justice, and quickly. However, when the Son of Man comes, will he find faith on the earth?"
>
> (Luke 18:6–8)

*The contrast: God and His elect.* The Lord wants us to recognize that the one to whom we pray is nothing at all like the unjust judge. He does not need to be nagged or manipulated into acting on our behalf. His care for our needs is not generated by our wearing Him out with our requests. Our persistence in prayer does not change Him or make Him more willing to act. We only pray properly when we think of

God properly as One who answers for our good consistently with His own glory.

We also need to remember that we are not helpless widows with no standing before God and no weapon but our persistence. We are God's chosen ones. We are participants in God's eternal plan—the children of grace. We may not understand all the nuances of God's election, but we can be sure that God's sovereign choice gives us a position of confidence and security. We are also chosen for a purpose. As T. W. Manson observes, the elect "are not the pampered darlings of Providence, but the *corps d'elite* in the army of the living God" (*The Sayings of Jesus*, p. 141). Since we are the chosen, the citizens of the kingdom, the children of the Father, we can pray with confidence. If a helpless widow who had no weapon but her persistence could get her way with a hardhearted, unjust judge, how much more will God's people receive what they need from a gracious Father!

*Our character: crying for help.* It is significant that the Lord describes believers as "His chosen ones, who cry out to Him day and night." The term "cry out" expresses something of the intensity of true prayer. A few verses further on in this chapter, Luke tells of a blind beggar who kept shouting out to the Lord Jesus (18:38–39). This was not a polite, dispassionate statement of desire, but an intense, urgent appeal to God for help. That is the language of prayer—the cry of the heart out of the difficulties and failures of life. And that is the nature of persistence. It is not a type of spiritual filibuster or a mechanical repeating of requests. Even less is it a refusal to accept God's no! It is the heart's cry to the Father out of the distress of life.

Several years ago I found myself in a West African country on my daughter's birthday. Missionary friends told me that there were only fifteen telephone lines out of the country, and to get an open line you just had to keep trying. For an hour and a half I dialed without stopping. Finally I heard the phone ring in Canada, but when they answered I could hear them and they couldn't hear me. So I kept at it until finally I did get through. Is that what persistence in prayer means—trying to get through? Trying to be heard?

We are not told why the Lord does not always answer our cries for help on the first occasion. Undoubtedly, part of the answer is to be found in the idea that God's timing does

not always coincide with ours. The unjust judge
delayed out of selfish indifference; the Father
never does. But His sovereign purposes are
not always synchronized with our problems.
Another factor is that we are not always fit to
receive what we ask for. Every parent knows
the difference between a child's request and his
or her capacity to handle it wisely. A teenager
may be sure that he or she is mature enough
to own a car or to set his or her own curfew.
A parent usually perceives things differently. It
is also true that persistence can be part of a
refining process. Delay helps me clarify what
I really need. It filters out passing desires and
intensifies heartfelt desires. Perhaps most of all,
persistence is part of the fellowship process. If
all I had to do was to ask God and then merely
wait for Him to deliver the answer, I would
never be pressed close to Him to learn about
Him and to get to know Him more personally.
The process of delay can be painful, but some
of the most precious experiences in life are
those times when life's hurts cause us to keep
calling out to God in prayer. As Campbell
Morgan observed, "The man who makes prayer
a scheme by which occasionally he tries to
get something for himself has not learned the

deep, profound secret of prayer. Prayer is life passionately wanting, wishing, desiring God's triumph" (Warren Wiersbe, ed., *Classic Sermons on Prayer,* p. 133).

*Our confidence: God's answers.* "Will he keep putting them off? I tell you, he will see that they get justice, and quickly." The Lord's promise is that He will vindicate His people and that all wrongs will be put right. However, there are two problems with His promise as it is presented here in Luke. One involves the translation, "Will he keep putting them off?" Interpreters have exercised their ingenuity on the original language, and no solution is entirely satisfactory. However, the main thrust seems clear: the Lord will be patient with believers' persistence, and He will respond to their needs. He will not be like the unjust judge.

A more difficult question is related to the statement that God will grant justice "quickly." Suffering believers have not always experienced swift justice in human terms. And for many, vindication was never given on earth. They have died as martyrs or as victims. Even the Lord Jesus did not know "quick" vindication in His earthly life.

Apparently our Lord is thinking in terms of the calendar of eternity. Vindication for the Savior involved the resurrection. For us, He will answer our prayers, and, when we experience the answers, whether in time or eternity, we will recognize that they came "quickly." What is important is for us to see that the Lord never puts us on hold and forgets we are there. Delay is not a form of denial but a means of preparation.

*The challenge: enduring or despairing?* The words with which the Lord ends this discourse express not so much a question as a challenge. "When the Son of Man comes, will he find faith on the earth?" The Lord is not communicating despair or predicting defection. He is challenging His followers to endurance. The real issue isn't the goodness of God, but the endurance of man. God isn't like the judge, but are we like the widow? We can trust Him to answer, but can He trust us to keep asking?

The setting of this discussion reminds us that, as disciples, we live in the world before the kingdom comes. This means suffering, difficulty, and affliction. The realities of life in an alien world mean that pressures will tempt us to lose heart and to give up. The Lord is intensely realistic about that temptation. But the ultimate question is not whether or not believers will fail, but whether or not they will fail to pray. The diagnosis is clear: If we do not persevere in prayer, we will not persevere in obedience. When we believers stop being those who "cry out to him day and night," we deny our essential nature as God's elect. Persistent prayer is the very essence of the life of faith.

D. L. Moody once observed that most people's prayers should be "cut off at both ends and set on fire in the middle." People who pray as if that has been done not only persist in faith, they persevere through life.

# CHAPTER ELEVEN

# SEEING MYSELF

To live for the moment is the prevailing passion—to live for yourself, not for your predecessors or posterity." Little has changed since Christopher Lasch wrote those words describing Western society in 1979 in *The Culture of Narcissism*. Little has happened to challenge his observation that "self-absorption is the climate of contemporary society."

As our society moves increasingly away from biblical roots, many forces conspire to fill the place most societies reserve for God with "self." Values are determined by such ideas as "loving yourself is the greatest love of all"; "I need to feel good about myself"; "I owe it to myself." "Self" has become the ultimate source of truth and value, and we are told that the answer to life is found in our self-esteem, our positive self-image, our unconditional positive self-regard.

Humanists, paradoxically, strip us of our true dignity as creatures formed in the image of God when they call us to affirm that there is nothing higher and more dignified than human

most familiar stories, the parable of the Pharisee and the tax collector, found in Luke 18:9–14.

> To some who were confident of their own righteousness and looked down on everybody else, Jesus told this parable: "Two men went up to the temple to pray, one a Pharisee and the other a tax collector. The Pharisee stood up and prayed about himself: 'God, I thank you that I am not like other men—robbers, evildoers, adulterers—or even like this tax collector. I fast twice a week and give a tenth of all I get.'
>
> "But the tax collector stood at a distance. He would not even look up to heaven, but beat his breast and said, 'God, have mercy on me, a sinner.'
>
> "I tell you that this man, rather than the other, went home justified before God. For everyone who exalts himself will be humbled, and he who humbles himself will be exalted."
>
> (Luke 18:9–14)

## A Parable for the "Me" Generation

As we have seen in chapter ten, the Lord Jesus has been teaching His disciples about prayer in the first eight verses of Luke 18. That theme obviously links this parable to what has gone before, but with an important difference. The parable of the persistent widow is given to the disciples to teach them to be bold and confident in their prayer because they are the Father's chosen ones. But this parable warns against a totally different kind of attitude—a boldness that is arrogance and a confidence that is impudence.

Luke explains to us that the Lord is telling this parable "to some who were confident of their own righteousness and looked down on everybody else." In the story, the Pharisee clearly represents this attitude, and, while this first-century group may have deserved the characterization, they are hardly unique. In fact, this is a very large fraternity indeed. As the psychologist David Myers has shown, the "inflated self" is a very common phenomenon in America today. In fact, when the College Board asked high school seniors to compare themselves with others their own age, zero percent saw themselves as being below average while sixty percent put themselves in the top ten percent in "ability to get along with others"! Myers concludes that "the most common error in people's self-image is not unrealistically low self-esteem, but rather self-serving pride; not an inferiority complex, but a superiority complex" (Myers and Jeeves, *Psychology Through the Eyes of Faith*). This is not to deny that, to one degree or another, we all wrestle with a sense of inferiority and deep feelings of inadequacy. But it is to insist that we are also characterized by pride, selfishness, and an attitude of superiority to others.

The people in the Lord's audience are "confident of their own righteousness." In fact, the Greek words Luke uses describe them as having a confidence *"based on themselves* that they were righteous." The foundation of their self-confidence was themselves. This is the common characteristic of all human-centered systems of self-esteem. For these first-century Jews, this confidence extended to their relationship with God; because of their religious deeds, they were righteous before Him. Modern people are less concerned about God than about themselves. Their goal is not so much divine approval as it is personal approval—"feeling good about myself." It is assumed that we are innately good and that our need is to "get in touch with our feelings," to actualize our true selves, and thus to realize the full potentiality of our human nature. Secular humanism tells us, "There is no deity. Trust your humanity." Cosmic New Age humanism tells us, "Humanity is deity. Trust the god within." To quote one New Age guru, "We are perfect exactly the way we are; when we accept that, life works." So, although their roads differ, the destination is the same. Whether it is the path of performance religion or of secular rationality or of New Age psychotechnology, the terminus is the conviction that "based on ourselves, we are righteous" (or "put together" or "self-actualized").

Scripture reveals that such confidence is, in fact, a dangerous delusion. All such claims overlook the basic fact of human nature— that humanity is deeply and inalterably sinful. Pharisaism, with all its good works and religiosity, cannot remove our guilt before God. Secularism, with all its optimism about humankind's "almost infinite powers and potentialities," (to quote one of its major spokesmen) "assigns to man nothing less than

the task of being his own savior and redeemer"
(Carliss Lamont, *The Philosophy of Humanism*).
But the salvation that it offers turns out to be,
in Bertrand Russell's own words, "the firm
foundation of unshakeable despair." New Age
mysticism, with its optimistic irrationality, can
sing bravely of man's inherent divinity, but must
close its eyes to the realities of sin, wickedness,
suffering, and death. When we are told—as
we are—that "all ideas of sin, fear, and guilt
are illusions" (Helen Schueman, *A Course in
Miracles*) we know that we have lost touch
with reality. When we are told that Hitler's gas
chambers were silly, but not evil, and that "the
conflict between right and wrong is a sickness
of the mind," we know that the inmates have
taken over the insane asylum.

The delusion of "selfism" is apparent in
another way. Despite all our self-absorption (or
more truthfully, because of it), our generation is
the most anxiety ridden, emotionally insecure,
and abusive society in human history. The
promise of the "selfists" that they would
usher us into a golden age of the individual is
mocked by the facts. People who "do their own
thing" not only erode their own stability, they
undermine the foundations of society.

Allied with this delusive confidence in self is a derisive contempt for others. Those to whom the Lord told His parable "looked down on everybody else." Yet, when self-worth is based on achievements—religious, philosophical, economic, or mystical—there is constant comparison with others even though there is no mutual respect. Elitism, pride, and a continual grasping for approval are common bedfellows.

Obviously, the Lord's story is directed to people who, as first-century Jews, would be angered to be compared with modern humanists or New Age mystics. But, while the differences are obvious, the essential similarity is far more important. The "self" has been placed on the throne where only God belongs. But what is the alternative? The answer is not found in cultivating an attitude of inferiority or self-abregation, but in obtaining a vantage point from which one can properly see reality. That is the point of the story the Lord now tells of two men who enter the temple to pray.

## A Portrait of a Religious Performer: The Pharisee

The term "Pharisee" has become a derogatory term, virtually synonymous with "religious

hypocrite." That was hardly its implication
in first-century Judea. In fact, the Pharisees
represented the pinnacle of Judaism. They were
deeply religious laymen, committed to upright
behavior and religious tradition. They were
highly respected by the general public as good
men. They cared deeply about spiritual matters.
But their fundamental religious assumptions
stood opposed to the grace of God embodied
in the person of Christ.

When this man comes to the temple to pray,
he is coming to his place to do his thing. He
is a religious man who feels very comfortable
in a religious setting. Standing to pray, as
he does, was the common posture, as a trip
to the Western Wall in Jerusalem today will
demonstrate, and it was not unusual to pray
aloud so that others could hear. None of this is
unexpected or unusual. This is what a Pharisee
does ordinarily.

But in one simple diagnostic phrase the Lord
explodes the pretense. Here is a man praying
"about himself," or perhaps the phrase should
be translated, "to himself." Prayer is meant
to be primarily God-centered, but here is a
man with an "I" problem. Because his prayer
is "about" himself, it is "to himself," and not

to God at all. His words lack any expression of praise, thanksgiving, or worship, and show no concern for who God is or what He has done. Instead, his prayer is disguised self-congratulation. It displays little sense of being in the awesome presence of a holy God or of a reverence that brings him to his knees, at least in spirit. Instead, he stands tall, convinced that he belongs in a class by himself, towering above others. He is impressed, not by what he is like compared with God, but by what he is like compared with others—robbers, evildoers, adulterers, and tax-gatherers.

What this man tells us about himself in his prayer would impress members of a religious society. The Old Testament required fasting once a year, the Pharisees once a week; this man fasts twice a week. The Old Testament imposed a tithe on one's income; this man pays a tithe on whatever he acquires, which amounts to a double tithe. Here is a man who not only does good and lawful things, but does them in a way that goes far beyond the requirements. He is an upright man, very certain of his own uprightness.

The Lord's portrait of the Pharisee is not a caricature. The Jewish Talmud records a prayer that may have originated in this very time:

> I thank you, O Lord my God, that You have given my lot with those who sit in the house of Torah and not with those who sit in the street-corners, for they are early to work and I am early to work; I am early to work on the words of Torah, and they are early to work on things of no importance. I weary myself and they weary themselves; I weary myself and profit thereby, they weary themselves to no profit. I run and they run; I run to the life of the age to come, they run to the pit of destruction.

Evangelicals have their own form of such prayers. I remember attending a Bible study as a college student and hearing a man pray almost weekly (such prayers are always easier to detect on other's lips than on our own): "Thank you that we're not spending a Saturday night drinking and partying, but we're here studying Thy Word and praying to Thee." His prayer was true, but he always seemed to be congratulating us more than conversing with God.

Now, there is no indication that the Pharisee's prayer was not factual. The Lord does not suggest that he was lying. What then was his error? First, he had *an inflated sense of self*. He was guilty of pride and self-centeredness, and revealed a blindness to his real position before a holy God. He may have used pious words and done religious deeds, but he had no appreciation of his true sinfulness. He was not praying to God, but worshiping at the shrine of self. Second, he displayed *a deflated sense of God*. His prayer lacked praise, confession, or petition. He was not truly in God's presence, awed by the divine majesty, but was in the presence of people, impressed by his supposed superiority. Third, he had a *distorted sense of values*. His focus was on what he did, not on who he was—on his conduct, not his character. Billy Sunday once said that a proud person was all front door: when you went in, you were immediately in the backyard. It was all facade. So it was with the Pharisee. Style was more important than substance; appearance, more important than reality. Joseph Kennedy used to tell his sons, "What you are isn't nearly as important as what you appear to be." This first-century performer would have agreed. Even in

God's presence, he could not explore beneath the surface of his life to see who he really was.

## A Portrait of a Spiritual Pauper: The Tax Collector

There was another person who came into the temple vicinity to pray, according to Jesus' parable: a tax collector. His reputation was the polar opposite of the Pharisee's. He was considered a traitor to the Jews, classed with robbers by the righteous, and shunned by the respectable. Tax collectors worked for the Romans and had a well-deserved reputation for dishonesty and corruption; they were usually corrupt personally and unclean religiously.

Whether this man deserved the reputation of his professional group is not stated. But his position and his posture reveal a man who wants to come into God's presence but feels profoundly unworthy. He stands "at a distance." That is, he stays on the fringes, as far as possible away from the Holy Place and from the place where the Pharisee has confidently taken his stand. His eyes are downcast, the body language of guilt, and he beats his breast in the well-known gesture of grief and sorrow. In fact, he is acting as if he were in the presence of death (Luke 23:48). Everything about him speaks of humility, brokenness, repentance. Here is a man who has no illusions about who he is or what he is like.

His prayer is hardly a prayer, but a cry of the heart; six words in Greek, literally "O God, be merciful to me, the sinner." He has not come to recount his merits but to meet his God. There is a sense of desperation. I do not know what failure led him to speak of himself as "a sinner," but clearly he has no illusions about himself. No excuses are offered. He knows that God does not forgive excuses, only sins. And he is also aware that only the grace of God can meet his needs. "Have mercy on me" has behind it the rich theology of the Old Testament. The term he uses speaks of a place in the temple, the mercy seat in the Holy of Holies, where sacrificial blood was sprinkled on the Day of Atonement to make it possible for sinful people to have fellowship with a holy God. This is not a generalized call for mercy. He knows he needs God to deal with his sin by making atonement. This is, of course, precisely what the Lord Jesus came to do.

Here is a man, then, who can see nothing in himself but sin and who seeks nothing of

God but atoning mercy. He has no interest in comparing himself with anyone or anything apart from God.

## The Principle of Approval: God's Courtroom

The Lord does not let this parable hang in the air, with each to draw his own conclusions. He wants there to be no doubt about His message: "I tell you that this man, rather than the other, went home justified before God." Please read the statement carefully. The tax collector did not go home "feeling justified" or "made righteous." The word "justified" is one of the great biblical words. It means "declared righteous," and here it tells us that God had not only forgiven the tax collector, He had declared him righteous and placed him in a right relation to himself. God the judge did this in view of Christ's death on the cross, which dealt totally and eternally with the sins of those who trust Him.

This becomes the great promise of the New Testament—that sinful people who trust in Christ "are justified freely by his grace through the redemption that came by Christ Jesus" (Rom. 3:24). This also becomes the great tragedy of the Pharisees. "Since they did not know the righteousness that comes from God and sought to establish their own, they did not submit to God's righteousness" (Rom. 10:3). Justification is impossible for those who are "confident of their own righteousness." Their self-images may be vigorous, their self-confidence impressive, their self-concepts well established. But it is all delusion and self-deception. Until we see ourselves in the light of God's holiness and God's gracious forgiveness in Christ, our self-images are built on a foundation of sand.

The Pharisee was wasting his time, "for everyone who exalts himself will be humbled." His religion was empty, his prayers futile, and his boasting foolish. Unless he bowed his heart before God in repentance and dependence, he could not experience the forgiveness and justification of God. The tax collector had come in humility, with utter dependence on God, and as a result had experienced the truth that "he who humbles himself will be exalted."

The Lord's parable was not designed to teach us the tax collector's prayer, a formula of words to use before God. The Lord wants us to have the tax collector's heart, a heart sensitive to sin and totally dependent on God's grace.

This is where salvation begins—with the humble receiving of God's gift of forgiveness in Christ.

But this is not where salvation ends. Humility is the way of life in the kingdom. The humble person is not a person with a large inferiority complex who continually degrades himself. He is, rather, a person who has accepted God's evaluation of his life. He knows he is a sinner, unworthy and helpless. Yet, at the same time, he knows that by God's grace he is righteous, exalted by God to full membership in His eternal family. As A. W. Tozer put it, "In himself, nothing; in God, everything. That is his motto."

When we see ourselves in the light of God's forgiveness, regeneration, and justification, we see our "selves" biblically and healthfully. Self-fulfillment is not the product of self-absorption and self-deification. To know God truly, to bow before Him humbly, to believe Him gladly—those are the pillars of a godly and realistic self-image.

# CHAPTER TWELVE

# GETTING MY DUE

Bill Borden was born a blue blood and brought up with a silver spoon in his mouth. His parents were both descended from British aristocracy, and his father had made a fortune in real estate in Chicago and in silver mining in Colorado. Bill was already worth a million dollars by the age of 21, an amount in 1908 equivalent to about 40 million dollars today. He was also handsome, intelligent, well-educated, and popular.

But in 1912, at the age of 25, Bill Borden did two things that made headlines. First, he gave away his entire fortune, half to God's work in the United States and half to missions overseas. Second, he chose to set sail for missionary work among the Muslims, first in Egypt to learn Arabic and then, ultimately, to a remote part of China.

To the public and the media, and even to many of his Christian friends, Borden's actions seemed incredibly wasteful, especially when he died of cerebrospinal meningitis shortly after reaching Cairo. He had apparently thrown away his money, his career, and even his life. To what end?

What makes a Bill Borden tick? What makes a person turn his back on virtually everything most people value to live in obedience to what he believes to be the will of God? What's in it for him? What are the returns on that kind of investment?

The book of Job records a fascinating exchange between God and Satan. When the Lord challenged Satan to consider Job as an example of godly character and personal integrity, Satan threw back an accusation: "Does Job fear God for nothing? . . . You have blessed the work of his hands. . . . But stretch out your hand and strike everything he has, and he will surely curse you to your face" (Job 1:9–11). That attack goes right to the heart of all Christian living and worship. "Hah! God, he doesn't serve you because he loves and trusts you, but because you bless him. Take away the goodies and the rewards, and he'll forget about you. No one serves you just because you're you!"

That accusation is powerful and discomforting and very modern. Just why do I serve the Lord Jesus? Is He enough, or am I held more by what He gives than who He is?

There is no need to feel embarrassed about God's blessings. Scripture does promise rewards and blessings for the obedient. But is that our motivation? Because if it is, our enthusiasm will probably wear thin in difficult times. Something deeper than the promise of rewards and blessings must hold us.

Satan's accusation thus becomes a penetrating question. Why do I serve the Lord Jesus? Why should I serve the Savior? And it brings us to an interesting discussion between the Lord and His disciples, in which He addressed the question of rewards posed by Peter, and used a parable to provoke them and us into deeper thought about spiritual motivation. As Matthew recounts the story, the discussion followed the Lord's encounter with the rich young ruler (Matthew 19:16–26).

## The Promise of Rewards: The Blessing of Discipleship

> Peter answered him, "We have left everything to follow you! What then will there be for us?"
>
> Jesus said to them, "I tell you the truth, at the renewal of all things,

when the Son of Man sits on his glorious throne, you who have followed
me will also sit on twelve thrones,
judging the twelve tribes of Israel.
And everyone who has left houses or
brothers or sisters or father or mother
or children or fields for my sake will
receive a hundred times as much and
will inherit eternal life. But many who
are first will be last, and many who
are last will be first."

(Matt. 19:27–30)

A study in *Psychology Today* in May 1981
probed the influence of money on people's
lives. One of its conclusions was that people
who are the most money conscious are much
less likely to be involved in a satisfactory
love relationship and tend to be troubled by
constant worry, anxiety, and loneliness. The
story of the rich young ruler, which immediately
precedes Peter's question, sadly but eloquently
reveals the power of money to control one's
life. The young man's tragedy was not that he
possessed wealth, but that wealth possessed
him. He would not let go of wealth to take hold

of the eternal life offered by the Son of God. His
trust was in his wealth, not his God.

In a society where wealth was often seen to
be a sign of divine approval and acceptance,
the Lord's statement startled the disciples: "It
is easier for a camel to go through the eye of a
needle than for a rich man to enter the kingdom
of God" (19:24). Salvation is not the attainment
of the rich or successful. It is a gift of God's
grace, freely given and humbly received.

But Peter was not affected by the drama of
salvation being enacted before him so much as
by the Lord's promise to the rich young man:
"Go, sell your possessions and give to the poor,
and you will have treasure in heaven. Then
come, follow me" (19:21). Peter's mind had
been riveted by the implications of "treasure in
heaven . . . follow Me." "If that is true for him,
what about us," he mused. "We've done that. I
left my nets and followed Jesus (Matt. 4:18–22).
What about my treasure?" Finally he blurted out
his concern: "We have left everything to follow
you! What then will there be for us?"

Only a person who is badly self-deceived is
hard on Peter. We may not be very proud of the
"what's-in-it-for-me?" feeling but it bubbles in
all of us, sometimes closer to the surface than

at other times. "It pays to serve Jesus," we sing. "It pays every day, it pays every step of the way." But sometimes the pay seems long overdue. We face fatigue, frustration, failure, or physical illness instead of blessing, joy, and fulfillment. "What's in it for me? When and how do I get some of this treasure?"

The Lord's response to Peter is not one of rebuke but of reaffirmation. It is not wrong to focus on rewards and eternal blessings, nor is it carnal to desire "treasure in heaven." The Lord often extends the promise of rewards in the Gospels (see, for example, Matt. 5:10–12; 6:19–21; 10:41–42; 24:45; 25:20–23). These are not demeaning bribes or the incentive programs of a sales organization. They are rather the appropriate results of a life pleasing to the God who "rewards those who earnestly seek him" (Heb. 11:6).

So the Lord directs Peter's attention to the millennial kingdom, "the renewal of all things, when the Son of Man sits on his glorious throne." This is the time prophesied throughout the Old Testament, when God would establish the kingdom of Messiah on the earth in power and glory (Daniel 7:13–22), and creation itself would become "new heavens and a new earth"

(Isa. 65:17; 66:22). This is the time all the disciples longed for, Peter no less than the rest.

Not only will the Lord Jesus sit on the throne of His glory in the new earth, but the apostles will share this glory. "You who have followed me will also sit on twelve thrones, judging the twelve tribes of Israel." It is impossible to describe how the twelve might have received this news. As Jews, they had longed for the Messiah, and they had staked everything on Jesus as Messiah. Their reward would go beyond their furthest imagining: When Israel was the greatest nation on earth, they would rule over it, as subordinates of King Jesus himself!

The promise made in Matthew 19:28 is, of course, a very specific one, made to the twelve apostles. But there is an extension of this promise to all believers. When Messiah Jesus returns, we who are His co-heirs (Rom. 8:17) will share in His glory, reigning with Him on the earth (Rev. 5:10). In fact, we will not only judge the world, we will exercise judgment over the angels (1 Cor. 6:1–3). I do not pretend to know all that this entails, but the promise is clear. Believers in Christ are the royal family of Messiah's kingdom, and part of our "treasure in heaven" will be to share in His regal authority and splendor.

But on what basis will this privilege be granted? In verse 29 the Lord establishes the principle of rewards. Present sacrifice produces eternal privilege. "Everyone who has left houses or brothers or sisters or father or mother or children or fields for my sake will receive a hundred times as much and will inherit eternal life." Mark, in his account, adds the fascinating words "receive a hundred times as much *in this present age*" (Mark 10:30). Obviously, the equation is not to be pressed literalistically. After all, who wants to receive a hundred wives or two hundred brothers? We could try to twist the statement into a formula for materialistic gain: "I give $100, I get $10,000." On that basis, we would be worse than the rich young ruler, and his tragedy would not be that he loved money more than God, but that he didn't know a good investment when he saw one! No, the Lord's point is to say that there is a blessing, both now and in eternity, that is out of all proportion to the cost of discipleship. Whatever losses following Christ entails (and there are losses—we leave things behind), the Savior himself will repay richly. Following may not feel like it pays—it clearly didn't for Job when he sat suffering on the ash heap. But in God's time and way it certainly does.

So the Lord summarizes with two points. "Many who are first will be last." From an earthly perspective, the rich young man was one of the first. He looked and lived like a winner. But in the crucible of decision about Christ, he made a choice that excluded him from true wealth. Those who look like winners from a human perspective are often life's losers. Conversely, "many who are last will be first." The disciples represent the "last." Uprooted from family and vocation, they wandered as the vagabond followers of a rejected leader. Like Bill Borden, they had taken a huge risk and apparently had come up empty. But appearances can be very deceptive. When they are seated on their millennial thrones alongside King Jesus, they will be revealed as God's first on the earth.

Peter's question has been answered. "Lord, what's in it for us?" "More, Peter, than you can ever imagine. You have given what you couldn't keep; you will gain what you can never lose." And that answer should be sufficient for every one of us. Although we do not see them all now, there are blessings and rewards. We must not demean this promise. But there is a troubling note to Peter's questions, which must still be dealt with. Behind "What's in it for me?" there lurks a commercial spirit that misses the essence of Christian living. It is that underlying attitude, present not only in Peter but also in me, that the Lord addresses in the parable of the workers in the vineyard, recorded in Matthew 20:1–16. The line with which the parable ends links it closely to the last phrase of chapter 19, which we have just discussed.

## The Picture of Rewards: The Motivation for Discipleship

> "For the kingdom of heaven is like a landowner who went out early in the morning to hire men to work in his vineyard. He agreed to pay them a denarius for the day and sent them into his vineyard. About the third hour he went out and saw others standing in the marketplace doing nothing. He told them, 'You also go and work in my vineyard, and I will pay you whatever is right.' So they went.
>
> "He went out again about the sixth hour and the ninth hour and did the same thing. About the eleventh hour he went out and found still others standing

around. He asked them, 'Why have you been standing here all day long doing nothing?'

" 'Because no one has hired us,' they answered. He said to them, 'You also go and work in my vineyard.'

"When evening came, the owner of the vineyard said to his foreman, 'Call the workers and pay them their wages, beginning with the last ones hired and going on to the first.'

"The workers who were hired about the eleventh hour came and each received a denarius. So when those came who were hired first, they expected to receive more. But each one of them also received a denarius. When they received it, they began to grumble against the landowner. 'These men who were hired last worked only one hour,' they said, ' and you have made them equal to us who have borne the burden of the work and the heat of the day.'

"But he answered one of them, 'Friend, I am not being unfair to you. Didn't you agree to work for a denarius? Take your pay and go. I want to give the man who was hired last the same as I gave you. Don't I have the right to do what I want with my own money? Or are you envious because I am generous?'

"So the last will be first, and the first will be last."

(Matt. 20:1–16)

Like so many of the Lord's stories, this parable plunges us into daily life in ancient Palestine. It is worth observing that the Lord was a student of life. His stories have the ring of authenticity because they happen where people live. We should notice that this story is not designed to teach us about labor-management relations or about salvation, or even about rewards. The Lord wants us to think about the attitude of heart with which a disciple should serve Him.

Day laborers were a common fact of life in the Lord's time. In this agricultural society, there were no labor unions and few contract employees. Men looking for work would gather at a convenient spot in the town's marketplace, and those requiring help would recruit the men they needed. A rate of pay would be arranged, the work would be done, and workers would be paid at day's end, in accordance with Old Testament law (Lev. 19:13; Deut. 24:14–15).

The story itself is straightforward. At six in the morning, a vineyard owner went into the marketplace to hire workers. They agreed to a fair wage and set off to do the work. There is no suggestion that they possessed any particular skills or abilities that made them more desirable employees than the others. They were available, agreed to terms, and set about their task.

But, for some reason, the landowner felt the need for more workers. Perhaps bad weather threatened the crop or a contract required immediate harvesting. More likely, he saw the unemployed workers and desired to help them. For whatever reason, he returned at 9:00 a.m. and saw men who were willing to work but unemployed. He made them a simple offer: "Go and work . . . and I will pay you whatever is right." They agreed and went with no contractual agreement, but simply with an opportunity to trust the landowner's promise and character. Three more times the process was repeated—at noon, at 3:00 p.m. and at 5:00 p.m.

When the day was done, the owner ordered his foreman to pay the workers, beginning with those who had worked for only one hour and continuing to those who had worked for a full day. When the one-hour workers were paid, they were astonished to discover that they had received a full day's wage, a denarius. Obviously, they hadn't earned that much. But a family could not live on less than a denarius a day, so, in generosity, the owner had paid them not what they deserved but what they needed. Apparently in his view, people mattered more than profits.

News of their good fortune quickly spread down through the line, and the twelve-hour workers excitedly anticipated receiving a bonanza. "If they got one denarius, we should get twelve!" By the time they reached the front, they had already spent their bonuses in their minds. Imagine their chagrin to discover that their pay envelopes also contained one denarius! This was exactly what they had contracted for (20:2), but it hardly seemed fair. "They only worked one hour and we've put in twelve full hours in the burning heat of the day. How can you call that fair?"

The owner's answer was straightforward: in effect, "It's not meant to be fair. You received exactly what you worked for. So your pay is absolutely fair. But I'm paying them generously, not fairly."

In the landowner's voice we hear our Lord's gentle rebuke of Peter. It is a warning against three dangers in the service of a disciple. First, there is *the danger of a commercial spirit*. An old rabbinic story is very similar to the Lord's parable, but the punch line is entirely different. When the protest is made, the answer silences the objectors: "This man has done more in two hours than you did all day." We understand that response. It is fair that wages earned should correspond to work done. Unions may protest, but we understand the equity principle—pay equal to work done.

But kingdom economics are very different. If we work for wages, we will get exactly what we desire, no more and no less. We become hirelings, dependent upon our bargaining skills. How much better to be children, dependent upon our Father's generosity. Our service does not put us in His debt. If we leave the reward to Him, we will be overwhelmed by His generosity.

Rees Howell, the Welsh coal miner turned revival preacher, had a heart to serve his Lord. Every day, after a long twelve-hour shift in the mines, he would walk two miles to lead a Bible study in a neighboring village, then return home to sleep. One night he came home in a downpour, completely soaked. "I wouldn't have walked there and back tonight for twenty pounds," his father said when he saw him. "Neither would I," answered Rees quietly. Money was not his motive. People like that don't need a salary, because they don't serve for wages. They serve an amazing Savior out of love.

Second, the Lord is warning against *the danger of a competitive spirit*. When the twelve-hour workers saw the one-hour workers and compared themselves to them, "they expected to receive more." When their eyes focused on what others had received, they were unable to receive their own wages with joy. Saul delighted in his victory over the Philistines, but when he heard David praised more highly than he had been, his heart turned to stone (1 Sam. 18:1–16). Nothing is less appropriate in disciples than comparison and competition.

Once, when driving with a friend through his home town, we came to a bewildering intersection with a confusing array of signals and lights. When I commented to my friend about it, he pointed to a sign that read, "Obey your signals." That's always good advice. I would love to evangelize like Billy Graham, preach like Chuck Swindoll, pray like George Mueller, organize like Bill Bright, write like Elisabeth Elliot, and sing like Steve Green. But those are not my signals. When I set my eyes on what the master is giving to other servants, joy evaporates. When I focus on His fairness and abounding generosity to me, joy fills my heart.

Third, there is *the danger of a complaining spirit.* "They began to grumble against the landowner." Such grumbling, the Lord reveals, is an attack on the goodness and generosity of God himself. Furthermore, it exposes the corruption of our hearts. "Are you envious because I am generous?" Who do we think we are to complain about the eternally holy, righteous God? It was the continual murmuring and complaining of Israel in the wilderness that aroused God's anger. Murmuring is an infectious social disease that robs us and all those around us of joy. Those who focus on their supposed deprivation and lament the cost of their discipleship have missed the wonder of the grace and generosity of our God.

F. B. Meyer once found himself involved in a ministry where the work of two well-known preachers overshadowed his own efforts. It was not easy to deal with the relative unimportance of what he was doing, but his solution reveals the response of a true disciple. "I find in my own ministry that supposing I pray for my own little flock, 'God bless me, God fill my pews, God send me a revival,' I miss the blessing; but as I pray for my brother on the right-hand side of my church, 'God bless him,' or my other brother on the other side, 'God bless him,' I am sure to get a blessing without paying for it, for the overflow of their cups fills my little bucket."

The Lord concludes His parable with a statement reminiscent of Matthew 19:30: "So the last will be first, and the first will be last." Here, however, the contrast is not between disciples and non-disciples. It is rather a reminder that external circumstances are not the key to eternal rewards. The "first," here, are the 6:00 a.m. workers. As someone saved as a child, brought up to love Christ, and given the privilege of ministry at an early age, I am much like those people. Friends of mine were not saved until much later in life than I, and their opportunities for Christian ministry are sometimes smaller than mine. Will those circumstances of life qualify them only for a lesser reward? No, says the Savior, emphatically not. God rewards the faithful heart, and generosity touches all He does.

Why do I serve the Lord? Because of fear? Duty? Prestige? Reward? Motives are never entirely pure, and a variety of factors propel us. But we are not hirelings, serving for wages. We are children, delighting in our Father's work and trusting in His generosity. Peter's great mistake was that he counted the cost and computed the reward without considering the privilege of service. On December 4, 1857, on the threshold of his return to Africa, David Livingstone tried to put into words the motives that shaped his life:

> I personally have never ceased to re-joice that God has entrusted me with His service. People talk a lot about the sacrifice involved in devoting my life to Africa. But can this be called a sacrifice at all if we give back to God a "little of what we owe Him?" And we owe Him so much that we shall never be able to pay off our debt. Can that be called sacrifice which gives us the deepest satisfaction, which develops our best powers, and gives us the greatest hopes and expectations? Away with this word. It is anything but a sacrifice. Rather, call it a "privilege!"

# EPILOGUE

Those who sat at the Lord's feet and heard Him as He spoke were astonished by what they heard. There was about His teaching an authority, unlike that of a careful scholar (Matt. 7:20; Luke 4:32). His words were loaded not only with truth but also with life. His stories and message had the power of authenticity. There was something else that caused them to wonder. They were "amazed at the gracious words that came from his lips" (Luke 4:22). His words not only had power, they brought healing. They probed the sinful hearts of those who heard and revealed the areas of need. But they opened a new window into the heart of our great God, revealing the full splendor of His glory and grace.

We do not have the privilege of sitting at His feet by the Sea of Galilee. We do have the privilege of hearing Him speak through these ageless parables and learning eternal truths about our Savior. The parables teach us indispensable truth about ourselves. But, unlike the man-centered age in which we live, they do not permit us to fix our eyes upon ourselves. The parables call us to know our God, to enjoy and to obey Him. Over and over, I meet a God whose love is unending, whose forgiveness is unfailing, whose power is transforming, whose ear is attentive, whose reward is unmerited, and whose home is open to all who trust Him.

I hope these chapters have increased your knowledge of the parables of the Lord. But a far more important matter is whether they have deepened delight in the Lord of the parables. The stories are wonderful; the Storyteller infinitely more so. Our world threatens to drown us in information; meanwhile our souls thirst for wisdom. Our deepest need is a recognition of the grandeur of God in His grace and greatness. In the God-centered world of the parables, we see life as we should.

May God in His grace give to you a delight in His person, a passion for His glory, and a confidence in His love.

# NOTE TO THE READER

The publisher invites you to share your response to the message of this book by writing Discovery House, Box 3566, Grand Rapids, MI 49501, USA. For information about other Discovery House books, music, or videos, contact us at the same address or call 1-800-653-8333. Find us on the Internet at dhp.org or send e-mail to books@dhp.org.